MENTAL HEALTH MATTERS

Kirk House Publishers

To Piper and Sam

MENTAL HEALTH
MATTERS

How Ten Psychological Principles Will
Enhance Your Mental Health

MELISSA MORK

First Edition
Paperback ISBN: 978-1-959681-47-2
eBook ISBN: 978-1-959681-48-9
Hardcover ISBN: 978-1-959681-49-6
Library of Congress Control Number: Pending

Cover and Interior Design by Ann Aubitz

Published by Kirk House Publishers
1250 E 115th Street
Burnsville, MN 55337
Kirkhousepublishers.com
612-781-2815

CONTENTS

INTRODUCTION

I am at the ER.

Man, I hate this place. I spent too much time here with my husband. For four months, cancer burrowed into his bones, causing him excruciating pain until he died. Now, five years later, I'm back.

This time it is even worse. My teenage son is telling the intake nurse his plans to kill himself.

I don't understand this.

An hour earlier we were enjoying a cheerful family dinner with lots of joking. Teasing. Laughter.

The food wasn't great (it was overcooked, dry, and tasteless) because I had cooked. But we'd had fun. We'd played board games.

We'd reminisced about the holidays. Conversation flowed easily. It all felt... happy.

Then, as we were putting the last board game away, he said, "Okay, I gotta go. Either I'm driving myself to the ER tonight, or I'm going to die."

My daughter and I sat staring at him in stunned silence.

Piper: "Are you joking?"

Sam: "I am dead serious."

I insisted on driving him.

Now I stand here, listening to my beautiful boy describe his imminent death to a stranger in scrubs. When I glance down at my shirt, there are huge wet spots on my chest. I didn't realize I have been crying since we left the house.

I look around the large waiting area, packed with people in hospital-grade masks. Every seat is filled. Folks standing around, leaning against walls, lying on the floor, sitting in wheelchairs. Most are wearing their parkas and winter boots and knitted caps; a few are wrapped in thin white hospital blankets.

Aside from my son's terrible words, all I hear is coughing.

It's the sixth of January in Minneapolis. We have entered the post-holiday COVID surge. It takes three days for my son to get a bed.

I stand here, in this awful place, overcrowded with people in masks. I know a few of them will never leave; they just don't know it yet. They are staring down their mortality in the same room as my son.

Their physical health is in crisis. They are facing a potentially deadly event.

My son's mental health is in crisis. He is facing a potentially deadly event.

My son speaks the words out loud to the nurse: "If you don't help me, I am going to kill myself."

In that moment, I fully understood this truth:

Mental. Health. Matters.

It's not like I didn't already *know* this! I specialize in mental health, for goodness' sake. Some people would say I am an expert.

I have a doctorate in clinical and forensic psychology. I am a tenured professor in a psychology department. I spent 15 years as the department chair.

I teach classes on psychopathology at the graduate level. I've conducted neuropsychological assessments at a nearby medical school. I am an advisor for doctoral dissertations in mental health research at multiple universities.

I am also a psychotherapist. I see patients at a clinic part-time. I do crisis interventions with communities after mass shootings. I host a podcast on mental health that has thousands of downloads around the world from South Korea to the Russian Federation. I am an international coach and consultant on mental illness, and I speak to international audiences on the topic of mental health.

Of course I know mental health matters.

Well, I mean, I knew this from a professional perspective.

But now it is real. This is not an academic pursuit. My child's life is on the line. He wants to die.

I felt like that neuroscientist Jill Bolte Taylor, who had a massive stroke. She watched as her own brain started to shut down.

I'm a mental health expert who is watching my son's mental health shut down.

My expertise is being called into play, but I am not able to apply it. This is too personal. At this moment, I am not a psychologist. I am his mother.

THE CRISIS

My son isn't alone. We are a nation in a mental health crisis.

This crisis isn't a surprise to you. You likely have someone in your family who has a diagnosis, or you personally have symptoms of a mental illness.

I know this because we are reaching a new level of mental illness in our country. In 2021, one in five adults had a diagnosable mental illness. Now we are closer to one in four. That's 25% of us.

In recent years, it's gotten worse globally too. In 2019, one in every eight people around the world were living with a mental illness. In 2020—perhaps related to issues tied to the COVID-19 pandemic—there was a 27% rise in anxiety and major depressive disorders. That is a huge increase in just one year.

In 2023, 45% of respondents in a US survey reported some kind of mental illness. Broken down by age, the 18–34-year-old age group has the highest rate of mental illness: 50 percent.

These are our emerging adults, launching into careers and vocations, getting married, becoming new parents. Mental illness is directly affecting HALF of them.

Mental health is a concern for many adults, but our kids are also in crisis. Adolescent anxiety is higher now than it was in the average psych ward patient in the 1950s.

In 2021, the American Academy of Pediatrics, the American Academy of Child and Adolescent Psychiatry, and the Children's Hospital Association joined together to declare children's mental health a National State of Emergency.

I will repeat this: children's mental health has been declared a *National State of Emergency*!

But for me that day in the ER, scholarly statistics no longer mattered. These data have no bearing on my life. Numbers mean nothing when my child's life is at stake. I could lose him to this crisis.

When it comes down to it, numbers don't matter to you either. Mental illness around the world is not your current worry. You picked up this book to learn about *your own* mental health. This is your highest concern.

Illness vs. Health

Since that night in the ER, my life has become a masterclass in mental health. I study it through a new lens. I am no longer interested in factors and statistics of psychopathology. I am not memorizing new diagnostic criteria for mental illnesses. Now I study coping and resilience and post-traumatic growth.

In the past, I had specialized in mental *illness*. I had overlooked factors of mental *health*.

I was so invested in treating the disease, I hadn't focused on prevention. I didn't investigate the practical strategies for well-being, mental wellness, or mental health hygiene.

That is a strange phrase, I know. Mental health hygiene?

You are familiar with the concept of hygiene: you keep your leftovers refrigerated. You avoid eating rare chicken. You wash your hands to avoid transmission of viruses. You brush your teeth to keep them healthy. You shower or bathe to stay clean.

You take multivitamins. You try to consume more water than coffee. Perhaps you try to eat something green every day. You walk or you stretch. Maybe you exercise. You try to get sufficient sleep. You get vaccinated to prevent some of the more debilitating viruses from taking hold.

When you cut your finger, you clean the area and bandage it to protect the wound. You prevent it from festering. Maybe you get stitches. You try to help it heal.

You go to a medical professional when you are feeling sick. You go to the ER if you are severely injured. You seek out a medical specialist if you have worrisome symptoms that could indicate a more serious issue. These are all exercises in good physical hygiene.

Even if you have a chronic illness, you continue to manage your physical health in other areas. You maintain your hygiene practices. For example, if you have an autoimmune disease, you still schedule an annual exam by a physician to monitor the other areas of your health.

In short, you use prevention strategies to protect your body.

But what are your prevention strategies to protect your mind? You manage your physical health well. Do you manage your mental health as well?

Physical illness is illness. Mental illness is illness. Physical health is health. Mental health is health. Good physical health hygiene protects your body. Mental health hygiene protects your mind.

This book is all about your good mental health hygiene. Together we will develop some strategies.

Situational vs. Psychological

But what if you already have some worrisome symptoms? How do you know if these symptoms are a mental illness? Could they just be a reaction to life's stressors, or should you get them looked at?

Here is an example. My client is deeply sad. They have no appetite, and they're losing weight. Their energy is low, they feel chronically exhausted and heavy.

They have trouble sleeping. They can't fall asleep because their mind spins. They can't stay asleep, so they roam the house.

They used to smile and laugh easily. Now they can't remember the last time they laughed. They have missed a lot of work. They've stopped doing fun things. They are withdrawing from friends.

Is my client depressed, or are they grieving? It looks the same. But each has very different causes, and we treat each one differently.

Depression can be treated well with a combination of psychotherapy and medication. We also recommend aerobic exercise for 30 minutes a day and altruistic activities each week, like volunteering at a food shelf or helping at an after-school reading program.

This doesn't work for grief. Grief cannot be medicated. It requires a very different process to address and manage it. Grief requires actual grief work.

Depression is a psychological ailment. Grief is a response to a situation. Most of the time, a problem you are having is due to a situation. What you are feeling is the reaction.

You don't like your boss because they are making your job harder than it needs to be. This is the situation. Because of this, you are cranky, prickly, and want to avoid work. This is your reaction.

You have a hard argument with your partner. This is the situation. You feel angry, panicky, and you don't really want to be around them. This is your reaction.

You get the idea.

Your emotions are a response to the situation. If the leadership at your job changed, you wouldn't feel this way anymore. When you and your partner make up, your emotions will resolve.

However, you may notice your emotions are not situational. Your emotions feel odd, unreasonable, intense, or distressing, and you can't point to just one event that may be causing this change in you.

I want you to attend to those changes.

The Four D's

In my field, I often look at a person's experience that brings them in to seem me through the lens of what we call the Four D's. It this experience different (or deviant), distressing, dysfunctional, and/or dangerous? I evaluate these on a scale of one to ten.

Different

What if your behavior is *different* from how you usually act? What if you are sleeping more, eating less, feeling jittery, yelling at others, driving more aggressively? What if you are crying a lot and you don't know why?

People who know you fairly well might say, "This isn't like you." You might even be thinking this about yourself.

If you feel different from how you have usually been in the past, pay attention. If this difference isn't in response to an identifiable situation, it's time to take notice.

If you are suddenly feeling a lot of panic because you just lost your job, the panic may be normal. But if you're feeling a lot of panic and can't point to a cause, and this is a new experience for you, then it is different or deviant from your norm.

Distressing

Symptoms of a mental illness are usually *distressing*. Your emotions might feel intolerable to you. You feel like you are going crazy.

Or these symptoms might be distressing for your loved ones. Your angry outbursts are scaring your partner or your kids. Your depressive symptoms are causing you to pull away from your loved ones. Perhaps you are having thoughts that are intrusive, unwanted, or upsetting.

When a client is having symptoms that are different from their norm and are also distressing to them, we will think about a possible diagnosis.

Dysfunctional

Mental illness symptoms can also be *dysfunctional*. They cause you to act in ways that don't help you move forward in your life. They keep you stuck, or they pull you farther away from your goals.

Your distractibility gets in the way of your doing your homework. Your panic keeps you from going to work. Your irritability is fracturing your relationship with your teen daughter. Your drinking stops you from being able to drive to get your son from a sleepover when he gets homesick.

When your symptoms are dysfunctional, when they get in the way of you being able to fulfill your normal roles, we will seriously consider a diagnosis.

Dangerous

Finally, symptoms of mental illness can be *dangerous*. Some disorders are downright deadly. The death rate for anorexia, for example, is the highest mortality rate of all mental illness.

Other mental illnesses—like intermittent explosive disorder, for example—can be dangerous when symptoms lead to interpersonal violence. Some disorders entail risky, impulsive behavior.

To be clear, self-inflicted violent behaviors—such as cutting, puncturing, punching, or burning oneself—are certainly dangerous, but we know this is less an attempt to die and more a coping strategy to deal with life.

When we think about dangerousness of mental illness, we are most concerned with thoughts of suicide. It is uncommon to see someone with a mental illness having thoughts of hurting another person. Individuals with mental illness tend to be victims of violence rather than perpetrators of it.

Suicidality is the greatest concern here. If your behavior is creating a risk of death, we want to see you.

To summarize:

- Are your thoughts, emotions, and/or behaviors *different* from how you usually think, feel or act?
- Are your thoughts, emotions, and/or behaviors *distressing* or upsetting to you or to others?
- Are your thoughts, emotions, and/or behaviors *dysfunctional* or getting in the way of you doing what you are supposed to do?
- Are your thoughts, emotions, and/or behaviors *dangerous?*

We look at these Four D's to determine if a diagnosis is warranted. On a scale of 1-10, with ten being the worst you've ever been, higher numbers on any of these scales mean it's time to talk to someone.

These Four D's indicate a possible mental illness. I have a QR code and link in the back of this book to psychologytoday.com for you to find a therapist in your area.

Developing Good Mental Health

Mental health is the opposite of mental illness. What does mental health look like?

Mental health is the state of being well. It involves resilience, self-awareness, good coping strategies, and healthy relationships with family, friends, your community, and yourself. A mentally health person thinks rationally and logically and can effectively solve problems.

Someone who is mentally healthy will have interests and hobbies they enjoy. When something bad happens, the mentally healthy person finds ways to endure it, process it, and then learn from it.

Your good mental health allows you to treat yourself with kindness. You have self-compassion; you let yourself fail.

Being mentally healthy doesn't mean you don't have bad bosses and relationship conflicts. It means you can handle them when they arise.

I teach courses on counseling and psychological theory. These courses explore a bunch of psychotherapies, from Freud to the newer, alternative techniques. Each theory is different and, I think, useful.

While you might think these psychological theories were created for folks with major mental illnesses, that is not how they are intended. Most of these theories are used to help clients know themselves better. They help you navigate difficult emotions. They guide you to find solutions to life's problems.

Please note:

If you had a serious physical illness, you would never read a book as your first response to treating it. If you break your leg, you don't hop over to the library on your one good leg to check out a book on how to make a plaster cast.

Please, my friend, do not read this book about mental health to treat your mental illness. *This book is not intended to replace therapy.* This book is written as a guide for you to develop better mental health, even alongside your current treatment for a mental illness.

Indeed, if you are already in treatment for your mental illness, this book is a great idea. It will help you enhance other areas of your mental health. You might choose to bring concepts you glean here into your therapy sessions to discuss in greater detail.

My Hope for You

I would like you to consider reading this book as an act of extreme self-care. Regardless of how busy you are, I hope you commit to this process.

To make this a priority, maybe you can carve out a half hour at lunch or sit in your car for half an hour after work while you avoid rush hour. Consider making a date with yourself at a coffee shop for half an hour on Saturday mornings.

Move your socials into a less visible, less accessible file on your home screen. Instead of doom-scrolling at night, give yourself the indulgent gift of self-reflection. Reward your hard day with exercises in profound personal change. Give yourself the gift of transformation.

Throughout this book, I will use ten counseling theories to guide you. Each chapter will start with a title that begins with the letter *P*. It will also have a main question to guide you. Each word and question will reflect a particular psychological or counseling theory.

As you apply these theories in the form of questions, it will help you discover what you need, what you want, and why you have been holding yourself back.

To guide you closer to your answers, I will ask you secondary questions. I'll make a few points, tell a couple of stories. I'll try to work in a dumb joke occasionally.

These theories and your answers to these questions will reveal to you what is possible.

Your responses will result in self-awareness, self-compassion, self-forgiveness, and hope. They will turn your answers into a love letter to yourself (in a very non-narcissistic way).

I want you to finish this book with your chin up, your shoulders back, and courage cascading through you.

I hope you find your resilience, your power, your truest story. I pray you abandon your striving for perfection and embrace your authentic self.

For you, I want better mental health.

Preparation

To prepare, I invite you to ready yourself by getting in the right headspace for presence and focus.

First, gather your materials, block out distractions, set a timer so you don't forget to pick your kids up from daycare.

Then get comfortable, close your eyes, and breathe. Pay attention to the place in your body that needs to relax and breathe slowly again.

Next, invite God[1] to speak to you. Ask for help to discern the direction you might take for each session of reading and writing.

Okay, let's start by getting out a fresh journal. This may be a good reason to run to the store.

Ooooh! A new journal! My favorite thing!

But don't let my desire for a new journal derail you. You can always use that journal you bought a while ago and wrote in for two days before you lost interest in it and tossed it in a drawer. You know the one; you feel guilty every time you push it aside to find your stamps or your checkbook.

Ha! I just pretended it was 2006!

If you don't have a journal, you can use a legal pad. Or write in the margins of this book. Grab a stack of post-it notes. Use the back of some unopened envelopes from credit card offers.

Whatever.

You do you.

Alright! Let's get busy changing your life, shall we?

Consider the following questions with me. Take a deep breath, close your eyes, and ready yourself to brainstorm.

- I picked up this book and opened to read it. What am I hoping to find?
- As I begin this process, what do I long for?
- What are my problems that I wish would go away?
- What would be different if those problems were gone?

---

[1] As a person of faith, I sometimes struggle to keep my spiritual perspective out of my writing. I will not impose any of my beliefs on you, but at times I may expose them for clearer context. Please do not let this distract you from reading this book. If you have a faith, please access it as part of your mental health journey. Having a personal faith is a powerful force for good mental health.

- If I went to bed tonight and didn't realize a miracle was happening while I was asleep, what would be the first indication tomorrow morning that a miracle had occurred?

1
PURPOSE
Why am I here?

As I stood next to my son in the ER, I realized my child had lost himself. He lost his purpose to go on. He lost his will to live. The only option left for him was death.

Fast forward to today; he is doing better. He persists through the harder days. He understands the importance of medication management. He attends regular therapy for maintenance. He maintains strong friendships, he works out daily, he writes poetry as a journaling practice. We make each other laugh every single day.

He has regained some hope. He has a clearer sense of purpose.

I know, I'm starting out with a boulder of an idea, but I want to start with your "why." You don't just trek out to a grocery store unless you know that you need to buy something. We need to have a reason for anything that requires effort.

Friedrich Nietzsche wrote, "He who has a why to live for can bear almost any how."

This is a powerful quote. Maybe sit with it for a minute or two.

When fellow psychotherapists ask me what my theoretical orientation is (what kind of therapy I do), I excitedly say, "I am an existentialist!"

This answer is true. It's a great theory. But also, the word also makes me *sound* smart.

Existential Theory

Existential Theory addresses several concerns that I believe are core to your functioning. We existentialists ask questions around guilt—not just guilt about the things you have *done* but especially around the guilt for *failing to do something*.

Does that resonate with you? Do you feel guilty for the things you didn't do? You feel awful for the things you could have done, the love you could have shown, the words you could have spoken, the person you could have become?

Sit with that last bit. I think that is why you are still reading this (even when I launched into something as deep and confusing as existentialism).

Do you feel guilt for what you have failed to do?

Yes?

Ah HA!

You are an existentialist too!

Now you can lead with that on your dating profile to filter out all the people who can't pronounce the word "existentialist." (It's "ex·is·TEN·shull·ist.")

Existentialists also consider isolation a primary concern. You are isolated from others. You cannot be fully known by another. You are also isolated from yourself. You are never fully able to know you.

The first part is obvious, but the second is true and nobody says it out loud.

I suspect this unspoken truth resonates with you: that you don't fully understand yourself. I guess this why you are still reading this book, even after I suggested you call yourself an "existentialist" on Tinder.

Existentialists explore the fear of freedom—of having to make choices and decisions in the face of so many possibilities. What if you choose the wrong thing?

Now, I *know* you've felt this! As you are registering for college someone asks you, "What are you going to major in?" You freeze up at the thought of having to decide.

Did you ever look for a new job and not even know where to begin? What if you choose the wrong job?

Or what if you find a fellow existentialist on the dating app? What if you start a relationship with them and you miss out on someone else who might be even MORE of an existentialist?

Frightening!

Seriously, freedom of choice can be terrifying. Existentialists would say it can be paralyzing. This is why we sometimes get stuck in indecision. Freedom paralysis is having too many choices, feeling too much pressure to make the right decision. Ultimately, it's a fear of failure.

Existentialists also explore fears around death: you are born alone, you live alone inside yourself, and you will die alone.

Yes, we are a fun crowd.

But, you see, I love this theory because it digs down to the deepest conditions of living that we rarely confront, let alone discuss aloud with another. When is the last time you stopped by your coworker's desk and said, "Tell me your fears about death"?

Word to the wise: don't do that.

And yet, the questions about legacy and purpose are necessary to consider. Have you ever been a part of an icebreaker exercise that asks, "What do you want written on your tombstone?"

My favorite gravestone reads: "I TOLD YOU I WAS SICK."

My second favorite epitaph: a recipe for fudge. Apparently, whenever she was asked to share her recipe, the now-deceased woman would declare, "Over my dead body!"

Another way we talk about death in polite company is when we discuss "the dash." Have you heard about this?

When you visit a grave, the grave marker has the birth date and the death date, separated by a dash. That dash represents that person's entire lifetime.

So the question is asked, "What will be your 'dash'?"

But you see, this all boils down to the most essential existential concern: Why am I here? What is my purpose?

Your Need for Purpose

Viktor Frankl wrote one of my favorite books of all time: *Man's Search for Meaning.* I highly recommend the book, but only after you finish this one.

When he was freed by the Americans from a concentration camp during the Holocaust, Frankl wrote this book about the *one* thing that most profoundly impacted him in the camps.

What was it? It wasn't the atrocities that occurred, while those were horrific. It wasn't the losses he faced, although those were devastating. It wasn't the dark questions he asked himself as he starved through the freezing nights, even though they were endless.

Frankl was a writer, an observer. He watched those around him in this atrocious environment.

He noticed there were two main groups. There were his fellow prisoners who shivered and worked and starved alongside him. And there were the kapos: fellow prisoners who had been given some authority and special privileges by the Nazi guards.

You would think, as Frankl did, that because these kapos received crusts of bread and extra pieces of sausage, shoes harvested from the dead, and coats retrieved in front of the ovens, they would live longer. You would think these men would have a greater shot at survival.

Conversely, you would observe the other lot. You would assume the ones who walked barefoot in the snow to and from the worksites every day would fall. The ones in threadbare or no clothing would freeze. Like Frankl, you would think those with no food would perish.

You would think that.

But Frankl realized the physical conditions of the individual didn't matter so much. It was the internal resolve that sustained them. Those who had a purpose to endure were those who survived. And those—kapos or not—who lost their meaning perished.

His conclusion was that each of us, in order to endure anything, must have a reason for doing so. Remember Nietzsche's quote? "He who has a why to live for can bear almost any how."

What has any of this to do with you? You have persisted through this life for this long because you have a purpose.

What is it? Why are you here?

Now, my answer to that question has changed with each stage of life I am in. When I was a child, my reason for being here was to receive my mother's love, to grow and develop. I existed simply as a receptacle of learning and being loved.

As a teen, my purpose was to explore a bunch of identities, to try them on like Halloween masks, to figure out who I might be. I was on a journey of discovery.

As a young adult, my purpose was to fall in love, to get married, to launch into a career. When I had kids, my highest purpose was to be their mom. It still is.

Okay, this reminds me of a story. Bear with me. It is a long one.

A Long Story

I like to scuba dive for fun. Well, "like" and "fun" are both exaggerations. I never actually learned how to swim. When I was five, my older brother Brad almost drowned in East Twin Lake. My mother decided she didn't want any of us floating away, so she sent us all to swim lessons.

But when the swim instructor had the audacity to suggest I submerge my tiny little face in the water and blow bubbles, I quit. I climbed out of the pool, walked back to the girls' locker room, and got dressed. I was certain that girl was insane.

In middle school, I feigned "female troubles" for the entire 6-week swimming module. I was so convincing: holding my stomach with both arms, grimacing, rocking back and forth in cramping agony. My PE teacher sympathetically suggested that I should see a doctor about my "condition." Poor guy.

Despite not being able to swim, I decided to take up scuba diving to impress a boy.

Do you know how smitten you must be to strap a 40-pound steel air tank to your back and belt some lead weights around your waist and plunge 90 feet below sea level without knowing how to swim!? Boys.

To become certified as a scuba diver, you have to pass a number of tests, including a 200-meter swim. I doggy-paddled for 200 meters.

When I finally finished and climbed out of the pool, the examiner shrugged his shoulders, said, "I guess that worked," and signed off on it.

Much later, when we were dating, I made the mistake of telling my now-husband (who is a master diver) that "I used to be into SCUBA." He was so excited. And I was so smitten.

So now I am diving again. A lot.

Every time we are on a boat on the way out to a dive site, I ask the dive guide, "Are you sure this is a good idea?" Often, they will look me up and down, see my white knuckles clinging to the seat or to the rail of the boat, give me the side eye, and ask, "Are YOU sure this is a good idea?"

When we went on our honeymoon to Hawaii, we signed up for a night dive on Maui's Black Rock.

Black Rock. Night dive.

Yes, it is as scary as it sounds.

From Shaka Guide: "Black Rock is believed to be the place where earthbound souls enter the gateway into the afterlife."

Let that foreshadow the rest of this story.

We started with a twilight dive. In our gear and tanks, we waded out into the deep water to a rock cliff that plunged down about thirty-two feet—not too far down, fairly safe, and you can walk back to shore when you are done. No worries. Easy-peasy.

We slowly floated along this cliff face in the twilight. There were all kinds of amazing sea life along Black Rock: sea turtles, goatfish, pufferfish, tiny candy cane shrimp.

The twilight dive was an hour of amazing, beautifully fragile marine life. We finished at the far end of the cliff, turned back toward land, waded back up to the shore, had a snack, and watched the sun set.

Lovely.

After dark, we suited up again with the goal of doing the exact same dive but with the night sea life out on display. We slowly waded out from shore, strapped on our flippers, floated out over the ocean floor, and descended to Black Rock.

We had underwater flashlights tied to our wrists and glow sticks attached to our tanks. The sky and the water blended together into inky blackness. All we could see was whatever our flashlight beams landed on.

As we submerged into this watery portal once again, we encountered an entirely different world! The sea life was so different than what we had seen just two hours before!

Trumpetfish, boxfish, sponge crabs, spiny lobsters, brilliant banded coral shrimp! Under the beams of our flashlights, eels were chasing each other, roiling, slithering, dancing in front of us as though they were in the spotlight!

We were absolutely mesmerized by the complete transformation of the sea life in front of us.

What we did not realize was that, as we were engrossed in this spectacular show, the current in the open water had grown dangerously stronger. As we finished the dive, the current had become a riptide.

A RIPTIDE!

We had been protected from the current because we were hidden behind the cliff face, but as soon as we moved past the end of the rock, we were blown quickly away from shore.

Later I read a review of Black Rock that said, "Black Rock is an area with some of the worst issues. It can be a very dangerous current there, and I don't suggest trying it unless you really know what you are doing."

I suppose "know what you are doing" implies one should know how to swim.

Because it was so dark under water, we could see nothing but one another's flashlight beams. Our dive guide, realizing the danger we were in, immediately shined her flashlight on her hand and motioned for us to go down to the ocean floor. Once fully descended, she used her flashlight to indicate we lay our bellies trim (flat) to the ground.

Following her lead, with the current pushing against us, rushing over our backs, I pointed myself toward shore.

I used my flashlight to see ahead of me, and then I used it as an anchor. With as much force as I could, I plunged the flashlight into the sand. I pulled myself toward it, army crawling on my stomach. Right hand pulling, left knee pushing, left hand grabbing deep into the sand, right knee forward.

I held my ground, looked up, inhaled. Inched ahead.

Again.

Beam up, look ahead, breathe in, reach forward, dig down, army crawl, exhale.

Again!

Beam up, look ahead, breathe in, reach forward, dig down, army crawl, exhale.

Repeat.

As we neared the shore, our guide used her flashlight to motion us to go up to the surface and swim hard. But as soon as we did this, we watched the lights on the shore grow smaller as the rip tide blew us straight out into the open ocean again.

Nobody knew we were out there. It was late at night. The inland dive shop had closed. We didn't have cellphones with us. It was dark, we were in black water, and there was no boat waiting for us, searching for our glowsticks or watching for our flashlights.

The dive guide quickly motioned us back down. We descended again and started over: belly trim, flat to the ground, position yourself.

Beam up, look ahead, breathe in, reach forward, dig down, army crawl, exhale.

Repeat.

Beam up, look ahead, breathe in, reach forward, dig down, army crawl, exhale.

I do not know how long this lasted, this combination of descending, crawling, clawing our way back and then going to the surface, kicking hard with air tanks on our backs and weight belts on our waists, only to descend and start over again. It felt like eternity.

My legs cramping, the sharp burn of the air in my lungs as I tried not to breathe too hard, the sound of my dive computer warning me I was almost out of air...

I had never been more afraid.

But I had to survive. I had to fight. My two children were back in Minnesota, peacefully sleeping in their warm beds.

They had no idea their mother might never come back for them.

They had already buried their dad. They had no grandparents. I was the only person they had.

Thinking only of them, I clawed on. Beam up, look ahead, breathe in, reach forward, dig down, crawl, exhale.

Again!

Beam up, look ahead, breathe in, reach forward, dig down, crawl, exhale.

Frantically, my mind is screaming! Beam up, look ahead, breathe in, reach forward, dig down, crawl, Melissa!

Beam up, look, reach, dig, crawl.

Do not die, Melissa.

Look, reach, dig, crawl!

Fight, claw!

Dig, crawl!

Fight! Dig! Crawl! Claw!

They need you to come home, Melissa!

Their dad is gone. They need you HERE.

They *need* you!

I had to survive.

And guess what? I did not enter that "watery portal where souls enter the gateway into the afterlife."

I survived! My children were my purpose.

Let's all take a deep breath. There's plenty of air up here.

You are going through tough times right now. How do I know? Because life is stressful and you're doing it. Whatever it is, you're persisting.

Having a purpose—a sense of meaning—gives direction to your life.

What gives your life purpose?
I know. You're looking at the words, "What gives your life purpose?" and you have swirling questions of your own. You're asking, "What if I don't know?" or "How do I figure this out?" and "Why would she scuba dive at night if she didn't even know how to swim?"

Ah, but I knew how to crawl, didn't I?

Ikigai
The Japanese have a word: *ikigai*. Loosely translated, *ikigai* is a passion that gives your life joy and value. Your *ikigai* is your sense of purpose, your motivation for living. In essence, it is your reason for being.

There are four areas of life that converge in your *ikigai*: what you love, what the world needs, what you are good at, and what you can be paid for. It directs you to your passion, your mission, your vocation, and your profession. If you are curious to read more, I encourage you to look at the book by Liebermann and Garcia called *Ikigai: The Japanese Secret to a Long and Happy Life*. They describe it beautifully in a way that inspires. You should read it after you finish this book.

For the purposes of this chapter, though, I want to focus primarily on what you love and what drives you. Your vocation and your profession are not as closely tied to enhancing your mental health, although the state of your mental health will affect your vocation and profession.

What You Love and What Drives You
Have you been a part of an organization that has clearly stated their mission? They may have their mission statement on the top

of their website, on their letterhead, written in the marble in the front lobby.

The mission is a statement that reads "we exist ..." Sometimes a mission statement is a single, clear sentence. "We exist to build the best houses." "We exist to spread the power of optimism." "We exist to use business to protect people." These very clear sentences set the focus and guide the actions of everyone involved.

The value is that everyone who is part of the organization is on the same page. The mission gives us all similar purpose. We are moving towards the same goals. Purpose propels us forward.

I am on the board of Gilda's Club Minnesota. It's part of the worldwide Cancer Support Community to honor the legacy of comedian Gilda Radner, who died from ovarian cancer. Our mission is incredibly clear. We exist because no one should face cancer alone. Every one of us in the organization agrees with this statement, and we are willing to invest our time, energy and money into this mission.

Do you have a personal mission statement? I invite my students in an upper-level class to do this. They start with what they value the most (a value statement).

Then they reflect on what they want to be and do (a vision statement).

And then they make a statement of who they want to be, of why they exist. This is their mission statement.

Sometimes, to discover your purpose you can ask yourself, "What do I care most about?"

"What do I weep for when I am particularly moved (by a commercial, an Upworthy post, a news story)?"

"Where do I spend my time and money?"

Your answers may reflect your purpose.

Look at what is on your bookshelf. What you gravitate to reflects your inner longings. Fiction or nonfiction, your books reflect you. What do you like to read?

If you can do an accurate assessment of your skills and strengths, you might see your purpose there. What are you really good at?

And what do you love?

Passion

Sometimes we think our job or profession is our purpose, but that's not always the case. Your passion might be that thing that you love while your work simply affords you an opportunity to do it.

When my late husband Scott was alive, he worked for a company that sells white sandwich bread and snack cakes that often fill children's lunch boxes.

He was so good at his job, he won the title "Best in Sales," nationally, ten years in a row.

That's amazing, considering he was selling snack cakes.

But here's the thing. He didn't love that job. He felt he was contributing to the national obesity epidemic. He felt his work was pointless.

He was good at it; he knew how to do it; it came easy to him. But there was no purpose to it. He didn't love it.

What he loved was horses.

He rescued abandoned, abused, or neglected horses from dire conditions. Then he nursed them back to health. The sales bonuses and other monetary awards he received from work went directly to helping horses.

He'd start the rescued horse on nutritious foods, supplements, his calm demeanor, and a gentle touch. He earned their trust to the point where they would follow him around without a halter or lead rope. They'd leave their big round bales of hay to come to him when he called them by name. They would run in from the pasture at his whistle.

He helped them to grow healthy and calm, resilient and steady. He worked with them to become "bomb proof." They would remain composed regardless of startling noises or movements. He trained them to be ridden well, so they could gently carry the most fragile of riders.

When they were ready, he'd trailer them to the county fairgrounds on Tuesday nights. These horses were the heart of a therapeutic equine-assisted riding program. Scott not only loved horses, he had a heart for kids with disabilities.

The whole process of therapeutic equine-assisted riding is amazing. The horse stands still while a child with low muscle tone strokes the horse's withers. The horse lifts its leg when a kid with a walker gives the prompt so they can clean out the horse's hoof.

A child who doesn't speak will utter sounds in the big soft hairy ear of their horse. A child with challenges in large motor skills will hold a dandy brush. With effort and love, they will move the brush up and down the broad belly of their assigned horse.

Finally, the horse patiently waits as a child is lifted out of their wheelchair and placed on the bareback pad.

This 1000-pound horse, all muscle and sinew and strength, shows such delicate care. We don't understand how, but the horse senses the importance of the task. The horse understands the magnitude; it knows the fragility. It moves so gently, balancing this precious cargo.

Sitting atop this animal that stands 16 hands high, a child does sit ups. They throw and catch balls from up there. They spray water at their parents who are pretending to flee.

There's a lot of laughter and shrieking. There are plastic bags and popping balloons. Bright colors and cascading bubbles. Children cry. Babies scream.

Yet these gentle giants, once mistreated, are now fearless. They tread gently across the long arena, majestic and calm. These horses are the heart of this incredibly meaningful work.

This was what got Scott up in the morning. This was where he spent his spare time. This was how he spent his money. This was his purpose. Selling snack cakes was simply his way to afford it.

What are you passionate about? What brings your life joy? Does this give your life meaning?

Longings

Sometimes your longings give you purpose. Longings are intense desires that are remote and often buried deep within you. They usually reflect your search for happiness.

Some of your deepest longings are for love and connection. You long for a partner. You ache for a family. You desire a deep friendship. You want to be significant to others. You yearn for what you have lost. You pine for connection and belonging. You crave peace. You hunger for hope.

What do you long for? What have you never had that makes you ache? What could fulfill you? Might this be a purpose worth pursuing?

Pain

Another way to explore your purpose is to locate your pain.

My mother was killed on my dad's birthday.

My parents had one of those marriages. She was madly in love with him. He thought all her flaws were "endearing." They were so physically affectionate they had eight kids.

When my mom died, my dad was devastated. His grief reduced him to a skeletal reflection of the big, robust dad we knew.

One day he asked me, "If you ever go to graduate school, I want you to study grief. I'm tired of people saying, 'I know how you feel.' They can't possibly know how I feel. They didn't lose your mother. Please, if you can, study grief."

I promised him I would.

Seven days later he lay down on the cool grass of a warm spring day and died from a broken heart.

I studied the patterns, processes, and obstacles of bereavement (grief) for my master's thesis. Watching my dad suffer and grieve so hard, with no way to help him, was painful. My pain became my purpose.

Later, when my husband died, I had the tools to help my kids and me through that dark mourning. And then I was able to write a book about grief, teach classes, speak and coach on the topic. My pain continued to be my purpose.

Nietzsche is attributed to saying, "To live is to suffer; to survive is to find some meaning in the suffering."

My pain led to my purpose. What has caused you pain? Can you use it for good purposes?

Sophie, a high school senior, came home from school to an unlocked front door. Her small 12-year-old sister had arrived home earlier and walked in on an intruder stealing some electronics. He assaulted her. It was a brutal attack. The little girl didn't survive it.

While suffering the traumatic grief she and her family had to face, Sophie also found ways to cope with it. She turned to her faith. She located support from others who had also lost a loved one to a violent crime. She spoke with people in positions of power to increase punishments for sex crimes and violent attacks committed during home invasions.

Sophie took her story of pain and turned it into a story of purpose.

Application

Now it's your turn. Frankl writes, "To be sure, man's search for meaning…is an indispensable prerequisite of mental health."

You might already know your purpose, so this is a no-brainer. But like many, perhaps you have never explored the answer to the question: "What gives my life purpose?"

As you think about this, you don't need to carve your answer in stone. Sometimes it depends on what your role is in the moment.

When I am teaching, my purpose is to deliver content and to connect with students.

When I am speaking, my purpose is to inform and inspire the participants.

When I am parenting, my purpose is to instruct and nurture my kids.

My purpose as a wife is to love and support my husband.

Now if I pull this all together, I have a clearer picture. My purpose is to empower others.

This is my reason for writing this book.

So, what about you? Take a deep breath, slow down your thoughts, and ask yourself a few questions.

- What are my interests? What am I drawn to?
- What do I care about?
- What do I get excited about?
- What scares me?
- What emotionally moves me?
- Where do I spend my time and money?
- What do I read about?
- Where are my strengths, skills, and/or talents?
- What am I passionate about? What drives me?
- What brings me my greatest pleasure or joy?
- What do I long for? Ache for?
- Where have I experienced pain?
- Can I use my pain in the pursuit of a purpose?

Based on these answers, can you write statements of your mission, vision, and values?

- The value statement represents "What is most important to me?"
- The vision statement is an image of success. "What does success look like for me?"
- A mission statement pulls this all together in answer to "Why do I exist?"

Please note:

If you still feel stuck in answering these questions, please do not be discouraged. Like I said at the start of the chapter, meaning/purpose is a boulder of a concept.

Please keep reading. By the end of this book, you will have a much clearer picture of who you are and what you value.

2
PASSION
What do I need?

Your drives, your passions, your wants, your longings. These are the things that make life worth living.

Your purpose propels you. It pushes you forward. Your needs pull you.

Let us explore what you need.

If you've ever attended a psychology, education, or sociology course in college, you probably studied Maslow's Hierarchy of Needs.

Abraham Maslow, a humanistic theorist, proposed a theory that you have five basic needs. The lower needs are most important; they are necessary for survival. Each need is built on the foundational needs below them.

Maslow's Hierarchy of Needs

Maslow's Hierarchy of needs Source: Maslow (1987)

Physiological Needs

The most basic needs, the foundational needs, are physical. You need food. You need hydration. You need warmth and rest. You need shoes. You especially need cute shoes that strangers in the grocery store notice and rave on about.

No? That's just me?

But you get the idea: food, water, shelter, clothing.

When you don't know where to find clean drinking water, you aren't worried about your self-esteem. Higher level needs are a luxury when the lower needs are unmet.

But when you are assured you have access to clean water, there are other basic needs. What about some of the other basic needs you might ignore or even reject?

Can you think of needs you deny yourself?

Well, have you ever prevented yourself from using the restroom? You were too busy to go? Other things were more important?

I have a colleague who is constantly on the go. She hits the floor running each morning. She is moving, running, hustling, teaching, leading meetings. She eats a lot of protein bars. She is fueled by lots and lots of coffee.

But she does not allow herself to use the restroom. There's just never any time!

And when she gets home and slips her key into the lock of her front door, the urgency takes over. The immediacy of the need is overpowering.

She has lost two good pairs of shoes from this.

What needs do you deny yourself? For example, do you refuse yourself comfort? Warmth? Rest?

When I was completing my doctoral dissertation in forensic psychology, I conducted a program outcome study for a cognitive restructuring program for repeat offenders in a state department of corrections. In other words, I interviewed and conducted testing with felons in a prison about their criminogenic thinking.

I met with each felon in a private interview room on site. I never became accustomed to walking through the heavy metal doorways and hearing the solid doors slam and lock tightly behind me.

But there was something I noticed when I'd walk through the prison. There is an absolute lack of comfort allowed to the prisoners. There are bright fluorescent lights, no warm lamps giving off a soft yellow glow.

Even in a northern state during the winter, and while the temperature in the prison is tolerable, there are no sweaters for them. No soft blanket throws waiting to be wrapped around anyone who feels chilly.

To watch television, there are hard plastic stools bolted to the floor. The cafeteria has plastic stools bolted down too. The visitors' room: hard plastic chairs with stiff backs. There is no soft seating. The only place to find a soft place to rest is in the cells with a thin mattress and thin blankets.

We deny comfort to the people we want to punish the most.

Do you deny yourself comfort? Do you give yourself pain medication when you have a headache? Do you let yourself take breaks when you are tired?

What other physical needs might you be ignoring or denying? Perhaps you have turned off your hunger cues. You don't know when you are hungry anymore. And maybe you don't know when you are full either.

Because my primary form of hydration is coffee, I don't know when I'm thirsty.

Do I know when I am sleepy? I have no idea.

Isn't "Sleepy" just a character in Snow White?

What physical needs do you meet well? What physical needs do you withhold or inadequately meet?

How is this affecting your mental health?

Safety

The second level of Maslow's hierarchy is your need for safety. It rides atop the physical needs because basic biological needs must take precedence. We know parents will put themselves at great risk to feed their children. Partners will stay in abusive relationships for the financial safety: for the shelter of a home. They may violate the need for safety to meet more basic needs.

Your safety needs will include safety from warfare, from community violence and external threats. You need safety outside.

And you need safety inside.

You tack down your rugs to keep from tripping over them. You check your smoke alarms. You keep the hallways and bathrooms lit so you don't stumble in the dark. You use safety belts and air bags.

On the job, you promote risk prevention to keep you from having accidents. Medically, you seek safety from viruses and disease.

You seek security. You stopped using *Password1!* as your password to access all your accounts.

You did stop doing that, right?

But you need safety from personal or internal risks, as well. These internal dangers might include perfectionism or financial worry.

You feel unsafe when you have unhealthy boundaries. You are unsafe when you use negative self-talk or you compare yourself to other people. You are unsafe when you engage in self-inflicted violence or other forms of self-harm.

Is there a safety need you are not attending to?

How is that affecting your mental health?

Belongingness and Love

Riding on top of your physical needs and your needs for safety is your need for love and belonging. You crave relationship and intimacy. You don't want to "fit in" with groups. You need to belong.

You have a deep social need to belong to someone else. You desperately need intimacy. You want others to accept you, to want you. You need to feel significant. You need to matter.

There is an entire chapter later in this book exploring the importance of having others in your life.

Reflecting on the first three needs of Maslow's hierarchy, I am guessing you are fairly comfortable. You are adequately meeting your basic needs.

You have a roof and four walls. You have some food in your cupboards. You have clean water. You have breathable air. You have warm clothing, soft bedding, cute shoes.

You are safe. You are not facing external threats like chronic community violence or the perils of war. Maybe you aren't very nice to yourself emotionally, but you have at least one person who loves you.

But let's continue to explore. The next two needs are not so easily achieved: self-esteem and self-actualization.

Self-Esteem

There was a lot of talk about self-esteem years ago. Parents made this their ultimate goal for their children: to have high self-esteem. Books were written. Lectures were given.

Alfred Adler, in his theory of personality, believed we all struggle with feelings of inferiority. He didn't see this as abnormal. In fact, he believed this inferiority was a wellspring for creativity. Your sense of inferiority drives you to seek mastery, competence, and higher levels of personal development.

While not a topic of my own academic study, I think self-concept (how you see yourself) and self-esteem (the value you place on yourself) are indeed relevant. They are certainly related to mental health.

Clients who finish therapy and rate it as successful will also rate their self-esteem as higher than when they started. In other words, you will believe therapy was helpful if you leave therapy feeling better about yourself. Ratings go up when self-esteem goes up.

But what causes low self-esteem? There are myriad explanations, but one you can control is this: your self-esteem goes down when your *ideal self* is too far away from your *true self*.

As an example, when you meet someone new and attractive to you, you expect yourself to be socially adept (ideal self), but you end up as awkward as you usually are (true self). Then you get mad at yourself for "failing."

Your self-esteem took a hit because your expectations were higher than what you were likely to achieve. When your expectations are too high and your evaluation of yourself falls too short, you don't like yourself.

Conversely, self-esteem goes up when your ideal self and your true self are most closely aligned.

And how do you do this? Well, what you *don't* do is mentally abuse yourself for falling short. Instead, try to set your expectations a little lower to align more closely to the truth of who you are. What are you capable of doing?

What if I decided my ideal self teaches at Harvard, speaks to stadiums of people, and writes New York Times best sellers?

Boy, wouldn't that be amazing!

I have two choices when considering where I am right now, though. I am doing none of those things. I could hate myself or I can accept myself.

How can I accept myself for not accomplishing those big expectations? Well, I can accept that I never made these my priorities. I didn't set these as my goals. I never set up a plan to meet those unstated goals. I can't beat myself up for not achieving them. That was never my ideal self.

Also, the percentage of people who achieve any one of those is very small. Those goals would be completely unrealistic for this average corn-fed farm girl sitting here typing on her laptop wearing a robe and fuzzy slippers.

My ideal self can be more closely aligned with who I actually am. Can I embrace the woman who loves her children lavishly? Can I accept this person who is able to laugh easily in the face of adversity? Can I embrace that part of me that is a terrible cook? A bad driver? Can I love the person who has to search for her phone every morning before she can leave for work?

It's next to the coffee maker, Melissa. It's always next to the coffee maker.

Self-esteem is not about looking in the mirror and liking what you see. Self-esteem is not rooted in how others compliment your looks or if they think you are attractive.

No, self-esteem goes deeper than something so shallow as appearance.

Where do you find your self-esteem?

You find it in the areas where you feel most competent. You feel good when you step up to the plate and take responsibility. You appreciate yourself when you recognize your unique skills, when you value what you are already good at. In other words, you like yourself when you show yourself respect.

You like yourself when you get respect from others. You are right with yourself when you are right with others.

You enjoy your own presence when you are engaging in hobbies and passions that alight you. You appreciate your own existence when you are altruistic and attending to the needs of others. You value yourself when you are pursuing growth and personal development. Your self-esteem will go up as you move through this book.

And it's interesting. As your self-esteem goes up, you won't feel the need to get affirmations from others, because it isn't about other people.

When you live in your purpose, pursuing your strengths and skills, you will blossom. This will enhance your self-esteem.

A healthy self-esteem is necessary for good mental health.

Self-Actualization

The highest need on Maslow's hierarchy is self-actualization. This one is a bit harder to achieve. But this, my friend, is what I'm really inviting you to consider as you read.

To self-actualize is to realize and fulfill your potential. In other words, it means to thrive. To flourish with purpose.

While "self" is in the hyphenated word of self-actualization, this is an act of transcending the self. This is about getting outside of yourself.

If you flip back through what you've already read, you will find the repetition of a single word: You.

I've typed the word over 1200 times. In all of these pages, I have asked you to think about you.

You.

That can be a lot of navel-gazing.

I love that term. It comes from the Ancient Greek word *omphaloskepsis* from *omphalos* (navel) and *skepsis* (examination or speculation). It was the practice of staring at one's belly button as an aid to meditation.

In our current culture, navel-gazing is a funny way of saying someone is engaging in excessive self-contemplation.

But sometimes, to access your greatest level of mental health, after searching yourself, you need to look past yourself. In fact, you may need to transcend the self.

In Maslow's theory, transcendence means behaving and relating "…to significant others, to human beings in general, to other species, to nature, and to the cosmos."

You reach your full potential when you are contributing to the welfare of others. Research repeatedly shows that doing things for other people, for animals, or for the world can buffer against your own depressive tendencies. There is even neuroanatomical protection when you do things that are altruistic. In other words, altruism changes your brain.

I often encourage clients who are struggling with anxiety or mood disorders to volunteer at a food shelf, an animal shelter, a reading program for at-risk youth, etc. Doing something for someone else is a very effective part of their treatment.

You self-actualize when you respond to your calling, when you work towards your purpose. You self-actualize when you shift your focus onto others.

When you do these things, *your* mental health is enhanced.

Choice Theory

Abraham Maslow was on to something with this hierarchy of needs. William Glasser, the author of *Choice Theory*, also developed a theory around human needs.

William Glasser posited that we have a never-ending quest to satisfy five basic needs: 1) to survive, 2) to love and belong, 3) to be powerful, 4) to be free, and 5) to have fun. You notice only the need to love and belong remains the same verbiage as Maslow's theory?

Survival

Unpacking Glasser's needs a little further, survival refers to both physical needs and safety needs. Reproductive sex is also included in this need.

Maslow didn't include reproductive sex as a physical need because, let's be honest, without food, you will die. Without water, you will die. Without sex, you will not die.

You may be living proof of this.

Power

Now, power is a curious one, isn't it? What kind of power is he talking about? Think about this need as a combination of the two higher levels of Maslow's pyramid. Glasser suggests we have a need to matter in this world, to make a difference, to be competent and respected. This also fits with a need to meet our potential, to leave a legacy, to find our purpose.

Think about it. To feel strong and competent, and to find our purpose—all of this is profoundly powerful.

Love and Belonging

As I mentioned earlier, this is such an important topic that you will see an entire chapter dedicated to this later in the book.

You have such a deep need to matter to someone else, you will sometimes invalidate your lower needs to achieve it. This is why you will see some people subject themselves to maltreatment in relationships: they will violate their need for safety in order to maintain an interpersonal bond.

Freedom

Like you and me (the existentialists), Glasser also recognized the gravity of freedom. The beliefs about it are different though. We existentialists believe we can be frozen with indecision when we are facing too much freedom. It overwhelms us and we become stuck.

Glasser believed we crave freedom. We want to be able to move without obstacles, to be independent and autonomous. Glasser said we have a deep need for choices.

While Maslow saw creative expression as a facet of that highest need of self-actualization, Glasser saw creativity as part of your need for freedom.

You can see how Maslow, Glasser, and Existential theories share similar foci. Freedom is a powerful need, and creative expression reflects this.

Discerning Your Need

How do you know what you need? Sometimes you can look at what you argue about with your partner or family. What is the common source of conflict? We fight about the same things over and over, you know. There are themes that are unlikely to get resolved unless one of you changes or the other one leaves. Then you start fighting for it with the next one.

So what need is at the heart of what you are you fighting for? Are you fighting for money (survival)? Are you fighting for respect (power)? Are you fighting for fidelity? For support in parenting (love and belonging)? Are you fighting for autonomy or independence (freedom)?

Fun

There is one more need that stands out to me in Glasser's Choice Theory. He recognized your need for FUN! You need relaxation. You need relevant learning. You need pleasure. You need to play!

My sister-in-law died of lung cancer seven years ago. My brother grieved deeply.

He had been her sole caregiver, and when she went on hospice, he stayed by her side 24/7. But she didn't go quickly. They lived out on a farm in the country, and he worked from home. He sat next to her hospice bed on his computer in the living room for five months until she died.

Her time on hospice and his grief that followed was a sad and lonely time for him.

And then one day, as his grief began to lift, he declared, "That's it! I'm going to spend the rest of my life having fun."

And that is what he does. He has fun.

First, he went online and found a sweet, pretty wife. She laughs easily, and he adores her. They go on long bike rides in nature. They annually put over 1000 miles on their bikes. This is a big deal when you live in Minnesota and you only get six months of snow-free roads per year.

When they aren't working or riding their bikes, they relax at their cabin. They entertain family. They have bonfires with neighbors. They float up the Mississippi river on their pontoon and grill burgers off the side of the boat.

They have fun!

Several years ago, I took a sabbatical from teaching. My topic of study: the therapeutic benefits of humor, laughter, and play.

While doing this research, I discovered an entire group that does this! I found the Association for Applied and Therapeutic Humor (AATH). People researching humor and laughter? I found my people!

These are folks who work in very serious jobs. There are surgeons and pediatricians. We have a lot of nurses. There are mental health professionals, educators, scientists, even a few clergy.

And, well, yes, a few clowns.

But we are all serious about humor!

We all agree that humans can endure almost anything if we can find a way to laugh about it. In AATH, we research, discuss, and use strategies to enhance humor in the lives of those around us. We use positive humor in treating patients, teaching our students, working with colleagues, pastoring congregants, and relating to our families.

Viktor Frankl writes, "It is well known that humor, more than anything else in the human make-up, can afford an aloofness and an ability to rise above any situation, even if only for a few seconds."

I suppose I need to mention Sigmund Freud somewhere in here, so here goes. In his essay "On Mourning and Melancholia," a missive on grief and depression, he writes, "Humor is not resigned; it is rebellious. It signifies triumph …in the face of adverse real circumstances."

If you're interested in reading more about humor, my previous book is called *Bounce: from surviving to thriving through loss*. It contains an entire chapter on the use of humor in coping with grief.

You can also read books by Paul Osincup on rewiring the brain with humor, Andrew Tarvin about humor at work, Jennifer Keith and her G.R.I.T. method to heal trauma with humor, Brenda Elsagher and her journey of using humor to confront cancer, Michael Cundall and his humor hack for resilience, and Allen Klein's books about humor and grief. I highly recommend all.

Anyway, I really like Glasser's needs, and especially the need for fun. It resonates.

Where do you experience your need for fun? How can you indulge in it more?

Quality World

Glasser had his theory of needs that aligned well with Maslow and also existentialism. But he also proposed that we all have a "Quality World" that we dream about and that we carry within us.

I like to think of it as Glasser's concept of Pinterest before Pinterest was a thing. Your inner picture album are the boards with pins on them, but in your head.

Let's say you get up and get your kids off to school with tummies full of breakfast. They are wearing backpacks carrying their lunches and their completed homework. They are dressed in warm clothes that are clean and relatively well-fitting.

Let's be honest here: these are a series of remarkable successes, and you made them a reality. This is the direct result of the snapshots in your inner picture album: your ideal world.

There are certain things that you value or desire, and you have images in your head of what those can look like. Some are easy to achieve. Some are a bit more challenging.

Glasser created questions that help give you a clearer understanding of your personal Quality World. Are you starting to pick up on how psychotherapists love asking questions?

1. Who are the most important people in your life?
2. What are your most deeply held values?
3. If you become the person you would ideally like to be, what traits or characteristics would you have?
4. What is an accomplishment that you are proud of?
5. If you could have the perfect job, what would that be?
6. If you were independently wealthy, what would you do with your time?
7. Describe a time in your life you would call a peak experience.
8. What does it mean to be a friend?
9. What is brings a significant amount of meaning to your life?
10. What, for you, makes a house a home?

Your answers are the values that form the core part of who you are.

Satisfying Relationships

Finally, Glasser challenges you to examine your relationships. What are the dissatisfying relationships in your life? What satisfying relationship are you missing?

You might be stuck in relationships that are hard. You have more unpleasant interactions than pleasant ones. They don't meet your needs. They aren't validating. You complain about these relationships to your friends. You avoid these hard relationships when possible.

When you can't avoid them, you engage with the person in your relationship through bickering, name calling, or emotional distancing. These are your dissatisfying relationships.

Sometimes these are the only relationships you have. They all seem hard. They all feel dissatisfying.

But trust me with this sad truth: you will never find a perfect relationship.

Perfect? No.

Satisfying? Yes. A satisfying relationship is possible.

What does a satisfying relationship look like? It is a relationship where conflict exists, but you navigate it calmly. Where there are an average of five positive encounters to every challenging encounter.

A satisfying relationship has trust. Respect. A satisfying relationship is often playful. Yakov Smirnoff says the loss of laughter in a relationship is like a canary in a coal mine. It signals the relationship's potential demise.

How would *you* describe a satisfying relationship? Is there one that is missing for you? Can you create one? Or help one grow?

If you are in a relationship that is less than satisfying, but you want it to be better, please check my resources in the back of the book to help you find help in your area. Look for someone who specializes in marriage and/or family therapy because they are trained in rebuilding relationships. You can go alone to work on your part of the problem even if your partner will not. Changing your part can dramatically change the dynamic of the relationship.

Application

Pause. Take a deep breath. Eliminate distractions. Put on some peaceful background music.

Understand that some of these questions may be a challenge, and that is okay. Come back to the other ones when you are in the right headspace.

- What needs are you successfully meeting?
- Which needs are you ignoring, overriding, rejecting?
- When you are in conflict with another person, what are you fighting for? Respect? Control? Love? Resources? When you examine the themes of your conflict, they often point to unmet needs.
- What is your ideal self? Your hopes for your best self?
- How realistic is this ideal?
- How can you align your expectations a little more closely with your true abilities, aptitudes, and strengths?
- If you were to engage in your full potential, what would that look like? How would your life be different?
- What are some ways you've found to transcend yourself? Who (or what) else could you serve?
- How do you like to have fun? Is this good for your mental health? What other ways might you implement fun into your daily routine?

Finally, Glasser challenges you to examine your relationships.

- How would *you* describe a satisfying relationship?
- What satisfying relationship are you missing?

- Can you create one? Or help one grow?
- What are the dissatisfying relationships in your life? What can you do to repair them or resolve them?

3
PRESENCE
What am I aware of?

Where were you exactly two weeks ago? Can you describe in detail what happened that day?

I am not asking you for eyewitness testimony in court, but imagine I were. Would you be able to recall that whole day?

If you're like me, it's unlikely. The days all run together. And to be frank, I rarely pay attention. I must check my calendar to even remember what I did yesterday. Frankly, most of my life is a bit of a blur.

Are you aware of your life? And if you aren't fully aware of it, are you fully living it?

You wander through the day, dissociated from the events. You are distanced from other people, disconnected from yourself.

You get up and you check your socials while you sit on the toilet. You take a shower without feeling the water. You swallow your coffee without tasting it. You put on your clothes without feeling the fabric touching your skin.

You commute to work, get out of the vehicle, and don't remember a single thing about the trip. You are on autopilot. You move through your day, dissociated from your life.

And while you detach from yourself and your life, you are living in the past. You ruminate on what you did, how you failed, ways you disappointed others, words you used callously.

You are preoccupied by how you've been mistreated. You focus on what others have done to you, how you were harmed, abandoned, rejected. You feel guilt for what you did, shame for who you are, and resentment for the rest.

And you get into this loop. You keep living in the past.

But maybe you are also living in the future. You might be worried about what you might do to mess things up. You might be concerned about how you might fail, ways you might disappoint others, and things you are afraid you might say.

You fixate on how others could mistreat you, how they can harm you, abandon you, reject you. You are on guard, hypervigilant, always watching for possible threats.

You feel anxiety for what might happen and panic for imminent catastrophes. You try to prevent anything bad from happening by trying to control the future.

Every day, you straddle the current moment by keeping one foot in your past and one foot in the future. Does this sound familiar?

In what ways do you linger in the past? When do you over-focus on the future?

When are you fully present, completely focused, living in the moment? What does "presence" feel like for you?

Gestalt Therapy

Gestalt therapy emerged in the 1930s. A large focus of this therapy is to help a client be present, to be mindful, to live in the "here and now."

I know. You thought mindfulness was a new concept. But no. The idea of presence has been around for a very long time. In fact, mindfulness is an ancient concept. It is steeped in Aristotle's idea of complete activity. It is also reflected in some of Socrates' and Plato's concepts.

There are a few Gestalt terms that I need to describe here. Be patient with me; some of the terms may sound complicated.

Don't worry. They won't be on the final exam.

Phenomenological Inquiry

Phenomenological inquiry is a process we use to stay in the present moment. *Phenomenological* means paying attention to what is happening right now. *Inquiry* means asking questions. It is exploring your life and your emotions with curiosity.

Phenomenological inquiry starts by inviting the client to reflect on a recent unpleasant event. Choose something that feels slightly objectionable but fairly safe. Avoid recalling traumatic events.

For example, did you drive through congested traffic today and feel a little fearful or aggressive? Did you feel jealous of someone at work? Maybe you had a less than pleasant exchange with a family member.

Bring a slightly unpleasant situation to mind. Put yourself into that moment as if it were currently happening—not to you when it happened but experience it as your current self. Bring it into the here and now.

Close your eyes and sit with it.

- *How are you experiencing the event right now?*
- *What is happening in your chest? Your head? Your stomach? Your throat?*
- *What feels hard about this moment?*
- *How are you trying to withdraw from this moment?*
- *What feels okay about this moment?*
- *What do you wish to retain from this event?*
- *What emotions do you feel?*
- *What do you want to do differently in this event?*

There is a purpose for these questions. Sometimes we revisit memories, but we visit them as "the past." When we do this, we don't confront the emotional experience.

If you had a hard breakup, you remember it, but you are detached from it. You recall it through the lens of time past. This allows you to keep your emotional distance.

The invitation to the phenomenological experience, using questions of inquiry, seeks to change that. If you bring that breakup to mind in the present, now you have some options.

You may explore the emotions you have in that event. You can sit with the sadness and be curious about the relief. You can tolerate the pain or live in the anger for a moment. You can feel these emotions with curiosity rather than judgement.

Emotional exploration is a goal of this theory. I want the client to fully experience their emotions in the situation.

Sometimes you can't explore or experience your emotions because you have habitually blocked them. If you have stopped yourself from having a particular feeling, a Gestalt therapist would ask you to name the emotion, try to experience it, and then exaggerate the emotion. Push it to the extreme. Your anger becomes rage, your sadness feels like despair, fear is pushed to panic.

Your emotion may feel intense, but the Gestalt therapist will encourage you to sit with it. The temptation is to flee from it, self-medicate, or self-soothe. But experiencing it in a safe environment helps you learn to tolerate it.

Phenomenological inquiry lets you be curious about the emotion. You are welcomed to explore it, poke at it, look at its ugly underbelly.

Don't judge your emotions. Sit with them like a close friend who is upset but safe. They may feel intense, but they could never hurt you.

Sometimes you feel emotionally stuck because you can't talk to the person who is, or was, involved in the situation you are recalling. That person might be dead, absent, or unsafe.

Gestalt therapists discourage talking *about* the person who caused you the pain. Talking about them gets you nowhere. You get trapped in this cycle, rehearsing the same thoughts and grievances.

Instead, you are encouraged to talk *to* the person who caused you pain. To do this, we use a technique called the "empty chair." Imagine that hard breakup. Bring it into the present, visiting those hard emotions. Stay with them, even in their intensity.

Now, instead of talking about what your ex did or said to you, imagine your ex is sitting in that empty chair across from you. Tell them what you need to say right now, in this moment.

Don't focus on what you would have said, should have said, could have said back then. Speak what is on your mind right now. Don't try to cover everything in one sitting. You can do this exercise repeatedly—in fact, every day until it feels resolved.

If this is something you'd like to try, you can do it in the privacy of your room. Writing letters is also a good way to get your feelings out; just remember to stay as present with your experience as possible. Use words like, "I am feeling _____ right now." "In this moment, this is what you are doing to me."

If you try it, you might find it is an encouraging experience. Rather than trying to change the past, which is impossible, you can address what is happening in the present. This is wisdom because—let's face it—the present is where you live.

Emotional Awareness

You can see this theory helps you increase your awareness in the moment and focus on your feelings.

Now, forgive me if this seems like an elementary school lesson, but some of us do not know the difference between sensations, emotions, and feelings.

Your emotions start out as *sensations* in the body. Your forehead is tense, your shoulders tight. Your stomach is fluttering, your heart is beating rapidly, your throat is constricted. Your mouth is dry, your skin is cold. You have to pee. These are your physical experiences.

Your *emotions* are the way you label those bodily experiences. You might call it fear. You could describe it as anxiety. You might be extremely bored. Perhaps you could call it excitement. What if this is what it feels like to fall in love?

All of these would be accurate labels for that combination of physical sensations I just described.

Feelings are how we interpret those emotional experiences. They are our thoughts about those sensations.

I feel afraid: I am….

I feel nervous. I must be….

I feel bored. I want to….

I feel excited! I'm going to….

I feel love; I need to….

Gestalt therapists want you to explore the physical sensations so you can label the emotions accurately. When the emotions are accurately named, you can authentically experience the feelings.

In my classes, I will invite my students to write down as many emotions as possible in 30 seconds. They usually slow down way before the timer stops. Some will list four or five. Some get up to 14 or 15.

Then we look at the feelings wheel by Gloria Wilcox. One student liked this wheel so much, he bought a sticker of it online and put it on his water bottle. He said the rest of the semester, he and his friends had more conversations about feelings.

When you examine it, you will see there are seven main emotions, with more nuanced versions of each one. Because they are so nuanced, you can feel multiple ones at the same time. For example, when your friend cancels plans at the last minute, you might feel skeptical of their reasons, rejected by them, and overall, disappointed.

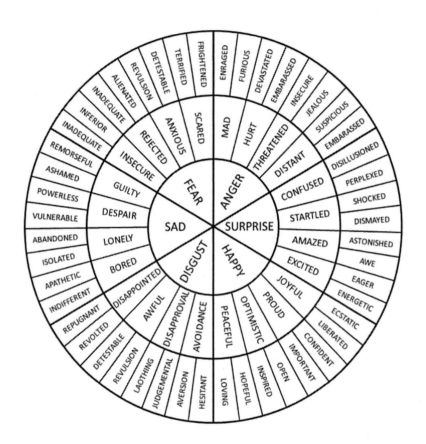

Similarly, this graph from Julia West is helpful to view five core emotions on a graph, scaling low, medium, and high intensity.

Intensity of Feelings	HAPPY	SAD	ANGRY	AFRAID	ASHAMED
HIGH	Elated Excited Overjoyed Thrilled Exuberant Ecstatic Fired up Passionate	Depressed Agonized Alone Hurt Dejected Hopeless Sorrowful Miserable	Furious Enraged Outraged Boiling Irate Seething Loathsome Betrayed	Terrified Horrified Scared stiff Petrified Fearful Panicky Frantic Shocked	Sorrowful Remorseful Defamed Worthless Disgraced Dishonored Mortified Admonished
MEDIUM	Cheerful Gratified Good Relieved Satisfied Glowing	Heartbroken Somber Lost Distressed Let down Melancholy	Upset Mad Defended Frustrated Agitated Disgusted	Apprehensive Frightened Threatened Insecure Uneasy Intimidated	Apologetic Unworthy Sneaky Guilty Embarrassed Secretive
LOW	Glad Contented Pleasant Tender Pleased Mellow	Unhappy Moody Blue Upset Disappointed Dissatisfied	Perturbed Annoyed Uptight Resistant Irritated Touchy	Cautious Nervous Worried Timid Unsure Anxious	Bashful Ridiculous Regretful Uncomfortable Pitied Silly

The value of having a vocabulary is that you can be more descriptive in your emotional experience. It gives you specificity of language. You can check in with your sensations, and then label them accurately.

Because emotions are so deeply nuanced, this vocabulary is helpful. It helps us manage our emotional responses to events. We recognize our triggers. We are better able to cope with our feelings. We know when to ask for help.

Also, naming your more intense emotions can help them feel more manageable. Naming them moves the neural energy dedicated to their intensity away from their neural centers and requires you to analyze, synthesize, even speak or write them down. Naming them lessens their intensity.

If you find this concept interesting, there are multiple feelings and emotions graphics available online, many free to download. Many of them in color! Order a sticker and put it on your water bottle. You'll get extra credit.

Unfinished Business

Gestalt therapists value phenomenological inquiry, questions that bring you into the here and now. They also value emotional awareness and emotional experiencing.

And Gestalt therapists will invite you to explore your unfinished business.

There are incidents in your life that you never fully resolved. When you bring them to the here and the now, they feel intense and frightening. These are the events that you try to withdraw from or escape.

In a later chapter, you will read about trauma. Trauma may be an extreme form of unfinished business. Much of our unfinished business, however, is not traumatic. It is simply unresolved conflict or painful exchanges with yourself or someone else that you never reconciled.

Your unfinished business is often experienced as intense discomfort. As you bring a past moment into present awareness, you experience emotional pain. Sometimes that unfinished business can even cause you physical pain.

Often, unfinished business will feel like anxiety, grief, guilt, abandonment, resentment, hatred, or rage. These emotions feel difficult, intense, overwhelming.

But what is causing them? Maybe you're not sure.

When you are feeling an intense emotion, you might ask yourself, "What was I thinking about just then?"

Your thoughts caused the emotion. What you were thinking about and the emotions that followed: together these can direct you to the event that is unfinished.

It is critically important that we explore these emotions that are tied to unfinished business. Left alone, unexplored, these emotions can create obstacles for you.

These hard feelings linger in the shadows, grow larger, and, when they become powerful enough, they turn against you. They build up; the pressure intensifies. They can develop into a mental illness. They can impair your relationship with yourself and, if they spray out at others, they can harm your relationships.

Your unfinished business from the past interferes with your connection with the people you care about. Unfinished business can cause fear and shame. Your fear inhibits your relationship with the world. Shame obstructs your relationship with the self.

If you can't figure out where your unfinished business resides, a Gestalt therapist will ask you to check in with your body. Explore your physical experience to see where this unfinished business is located. Is there pain in your chest related to being abandoned and broken-hearted? Are your shoulders chronically tight because you were always on alert as a child?

Molly is a survivor of domestic violence. The violence involved a lot of yelling, accusations, criticism, chest puffing, closed fists, door pounding, verbal threats, aggressive and reckless driving, even holes punched in walls. Sometimes, the violence escalated, and her abuser would push, shove, punch. Once in a while, he would lose control and choke her.

The relationship ended: her abuser had died. She finally felt safe.

Molly did a lot of work in therapy to overcome the trauma of the abuse: EMDR, Accelerated Resolution Therapy (ART),

Brainspotting. She even used Immanuel Prayer through her church.

Due to her intensive therapies, she could now talk about the abuse to her survivors support group without sobbing. She considered this a success! And it was!

And yet, in follow-up therapy, when her therapist mentions "unfinished business," Molly's fingers flutter to her throat. She has processed much of the abuse, but the emotions around being choked are still unresolved. The sensations in her throat and neck reflect there is more work to be done.

To do the work around unfinished business, especially as it relates to trauma, you might benefit from therapy. Reminder: I have included a section on mental health resources in the back of the book for you to find a therapist in your area.

"It" vs "I"

Gestalt therapists listen to the way you talk about the self and your experiences in the present tense. When you slip into future tense or past tense, they bring you back to the present. They will ask, "What does that feel like right now?"

As you talk, the therapist will also listen for specific words, like "it" or "they."

"It talk" happens when you use "it" instead of "I."

If I ask you, "How are you?" and you say, "It's been hard," that is "it talk." Using "it" allows you depersonalize the difficulty. You are dissociating from the experience.

How might you change how you describe the situation?

Instead of saying, "It's been hard," try saying "I'm having a hard time." We change the language. Using an "I" statement makes it personal. The "I" statement allows ownership, making the experience yours. "I" brings the answer into an active, present tense.

Another answer in place of "It's been hard" is to change it to "I'm giving myself a hard time."

As we say in Minnesota, "Uffda. You're telling the truth now."

Let's unpack that. "I'm giving myself a hard time." Using an "I" statement makes it personal. It is an active tense, bringing this into the present. And you are taking responsibility for the challenge.

"I'm doing this thing to me." Now there is something that can be done with it. You acknowledge your control over it.

When have you been using "it" instead of "I?" Can you listen for this to see if this is one of your patterns?

"I" vs "They"

Another language hiccup is "they talk."

"They will think I'm a failure."

"They will not like me."

Really? Have "they" told you this? Why are "they" being so mean to you? Do you need me to find "them" and punch them in the nose for you? Do you even know who "they" are, these folks who are so judgmental?

Chelsey had a dream of starting her own baking business. She had a professional grade kitchen in her home, so now she wanted a place to sell her goodies.

She saw a cute little space on Main Street that had just opened up to lease. It would be perfect for her new business.

She got a business loan and rented out the store front. Because people don't usually drive up and park just for pastries, she added coffee to the menu.

Quickly, the traffic was streaming in. People would occasionally buy her bakery items, but usually they just wanted coffee.

As her business grew, she was no longer a baker. She was a barista.

She was running a small business: hiring and firing, doing spreadsheets and taxes.

She didn't love it.

And she didn't love coffee.

She loved baking and decorating, but now that was relegated to late nights and early mornings. Payroll gave her ulcers. The roaring espresso machines and screaming milk steamers gave her headaches.

No, she did not love it at all. In fact, she resented it.

But she couldn't stop. She had to keep the business going. She had to do exactly the opposite of what she really loved.

Why? Because people would be disappointed in her. They would judge her. They would say she was a quitter. They would think she gave up just because it was too hard.

Our conversation went like this:

Me: Who, exactly? Who is "they?"

Chelsey: I don't know.

Me: Is it your husband?

Chelsey: No. He sees how stressed out I am. He wants me to shut it down.

Me: Are you concerned that your dad will be disappointed in you?

Chelsey: No. He's always proud of me. I think he would be proud of me no matter what I did.

Me: How about your friends? Would they judge you if you closed it down?

Chelsey: No, they just want me to be happy.

Me: Who are we talking about then?

Chelsey: I don't know.

She didn't know who *they* were, but *they* were terrorizing her with their demands. *They* were being mean to her. *They* were stopping her from doing what she needed to do. *They* were so cruel.

This generalized use of an "othered" pronoun like *they* will keep her stuck in something that makes her miserable. And her misery is interfering with her life.

But, by saying "they," you deflect ownership. Changing it to "I" is more accurate, more honest, and more manageable.

I encouraged Chelsey to try saying, "I will be disappointed if I sell it because this is what I thought I wanted," "I will feel like a failure because I will tell myself I couldn't hack it," "I will think I'm a quitter if I shut it down it," "I will tell myself I gave up just because it was hard."

Owning it helps you change it. Using an "I" statement gives you control. Shutter the business. Get a different job that doesn't keep you up at night. Go back to baking for fun, Chelsey.

When have you blamed "they" or "them" for your indecision or poor decisions? When have "they" kept you from happiness?

The next step might be to ask yourself, "What do I want instead?" or "What do I need in my life?" or "What will nourish me more?" or "What will set me free?"

Take control. Stop blaming "them." You can't satisfy "them" because "they" are ghosts.

We have briefly explored how Gestalt therapy works and the value of awareness and of living in the present moment. We have examined phenomenological inquiry, being curious and asking questions about your experience. We talked about emotional awareness. We explored unfinished business. We wrapped up with "it speak," and we discussed the tyranny of "they" against the freedom of "I."

Now I want to circle back to the present. Staying mindful, creating awareness, being in the here and now.

Activities for Greater Mindfulness

Did you know the average adult attention span is now seven seconds long? This is why TikTok algorithms favor seven second videos.

By the way, I love TikTok. Come find me over there!

But these short attention spans pull you away from your life. You miss the sweeter moments of life because you aren't looking for them.

I have a fun exercise that takes very little time and enhances your mindfulness significantly.

Savoring

In my Positive Psychology class, I give each of my students a raisin. I ask them to observe it with all five senses.

You can try this yourself: take a raisin (preferably a fresh one and not one you found under your toddler's car seat from last summer) and examine it. You can also do this with a bite of fruit, a peanut, a piece of candy, a crust of bread. Any morsel will work. For my students, it is a raisin.

Sight: examine the raisin and describe what you see. Notice the color, the ridges, the bumps.

Touch: feel the texture, temperature, firmness, softness. Explore it with your fingers. How would you describe the feel of it?

Smell: hold it close to your nose and inhale slowly. What does it smell like? "Um, it smells like a raisin, Melissa." Yes, I know, but try to be even more descriptive. Is it tangy? Sweet? Earthy? Jammy? Choose a few different words to describe the smell.

Taste: Now, put it in your mouth and roll it around. Do you feel the texture on your tongue? The firm little mound against the roof of your mouth?

As you bite down on it gently, what happens? Does the taste change? Where does the flavor start on your tongue?

Sound: Listen to your chewing. Focus on the sound as it changes from first bite to second bite to third bite. What words would you use to describe the sound?

Interoception: Notice the sensations as you swallow. Do you feel it moving to the back of the tongue, into your throat, down into your chest? How would you describe that internal transition?

Savoring is a mindfulness exercise to bring you directly into a fullness of experience. You can do this with almost anything.

Your senses ground you to your body, to the earth, and to your environment. Using your senses to savor a pleasant experience lets you be fully present with it.

You've never enjoyed a raisin so much as you did this one. Am I right?

What else might you savor today? How about your morning coffee? Savor the color, the temperature of the mug against your hands, the steam as it approaches your face. Inhale the smell, explore the taste, feel the texture on your tongue as you take your first sip.

How about the sensations of the shower? What does the water look like? How does it glisten? How does it stream? There are smells of the toiletries and tastes of the water, sounds of the water drops as they hit the shower floor. Notice the temperature of the water when it hits your shoulders, how it cools as it rolls to your feet.

As you get dressed, observe the colors of the outfit, the threads that crisscross to create the fabric, the lingering smells from the laundry. Listen to the sounds of the fabrics moving against each other. Notice the sound and feel of the friction of fabric against your skin. Feel the coolness of your bare skin adapting to the warmth of the shirt as it covers your back.

How about the sensory experience of a loved one? Your child as you hold her? The freckles on her nose, her smell of her hair, the tinkle of her laughter, her warmth, the feel of your lips when you kiss the top of her head.

Imagine how lovely it would be to savor an intimate moment with your partner. Suppose you successfully excluded any thoughts about what to cook later or what is on your calendar for tomorrow. You savor the intimacy as you exclusively focus on the sight of them, how they smell, how they taste, how you feel in the moment, the sounds you make together, the places in your body that feel the most pleasure.

Whew! Is it me or is it getting hot in here?

Yeah, okay. Go ahead. Put the book down. Go find your person.

I'll wait.

Morning Habits

When I wake up, the first thing I do is turn off my alarm on my phone. Since my phone is in my hand, I check my email. Then I go on social media and check my DMs and IMs and LinkedIns. I scroll to see who said what and where they are.

Then I hit the news. An hour later I have consumed a lot of garbage, and I haven't even had breakfast yet.

I love the saying from Joshua Sprague: *Create first, consume second.* He suggests we wake up and immediately do something that nourishes us: cook, write, draw, paint, exercise. Do whatever it is you do that is creative. Then you can consume social media and news and breakfast.

When you aren't going on your phone first thing in the morning, you can dedicate that time to something that is really good for your mental health. I mean REALLY good.

Julia Cameron, in her book *The Artist's Way* encourages readers to engage in what she calls "morning pages." These are three pages of unedited stream-of-consciousness, handwritten "brain drain."

Nothing is too silly, too inconsequential, or too ugly for morning pages. You are not allowed to judge your writing; you cannot edit. You just write. It doesn't have to be pretty or clever or pithy. No else is ever to read these morning pages. You can write whatever comes to mind.

These "morning pages" are often filled with negative spewing of interior garbage, and that's sort of the point. By expelling all of your mess onto paper, in black and white, you remove it from your mind for now. This affords you an opening for meditation and presence.

Meditation

Mornings are a great time to move you into presence. And you can do that through meditation. Meditation is not difficult, but it does take effort. This is why we call it a "practice" rather than a tradition or routine. You don't get perfect at meditation; you grow in it.

Here is how we start. Do this as you read these words.

Relaxation

Begin with your breath.

Slow it down. Feel the air moving through your nose. Savor the feel of air filling your chest and then escaping.

Experience the air expanding inside of you as you slowly inhale. Notice the air moving out of you as you exhale.

Observe your chest raising and lowering. Maybe your breath moves your shoulders up and down. Place your hand on your tummy. See if you can transition that swelling and shrinking from your chest to your stomach. Notice your diaphragm expanding and contracting with the breath. Can you hear the air moving in and out?

What smell do you capture as you inhale? Does the taste in your mouth change as you breathe through your nose? Is the taste on your tongue stronger when you exhale?

This is the beginning of your focused meditation.

As you breathe, shift your focus to the sensations in your body. Where do you feel sensations? Is your stomach growling? Does your throat feel dry or thirsty? Do you feel gas bubbling in your intestines?

Attend to where there might be tension in your body. You have slight pain in your temples. See if you can move the muscles in your face to shift that sensation.

Move your attention to your face. What is the position of your jaw? Is it clenched, or does it wiggle easily?

How about your neck? Do you notice tension there? Does it tilt easily forward? Back? Will you hover your head over your right shoulder? Then over your left? Can you swivel your neck around to loosen it a bit?

Now center your head directly above your neck to a resting position to reduce your neck's burden.

Holding your head centered over your neck, lift your shoulders up and let them drop. Again. Move them forward as if you were trying to touch them together, and squeeze. Do you notice the tension across the top of your shoulders or back? Relax and do it again. Where else do you notice a muscle resisting?

Squeeze your shoulders behind you as though you were trying to touch your elbows. Where do you notice tension? Is it across the front? In your biceps?

Systematically move your focus down your body. Where else might there be tension that could use a bit of release? Flex or stretch, hold, and relax the large muscle groups in your hands, arms, stomach, back, bum, thighs, calves, ankles, and feet.

In this process you are experiencing two senses we don't usually talk about. In the raisin exercise, I used the term "interoception." Interoception describes the sensations inside of your body related to pain, experiences of the internal sensations of movement, like gas bubbles, feeling hungry or full, thirsty, hot, cold, sleepy, or energized.

Proprioception, or kinesthesia, is the sense that allows you to perceive the location, movement, and action of your body. It is a complex set of sensations, like knowing the position of your joints. Proprioception is recognizing how your body is moving, your muscle activity, your energy, balance, and so on.

Focusing on the five senses as you breathe, and the interoception and proprioception of your body, you are now ready to focus on a meditation of your choice.

Mantras

Meditation can be a number of things. Let's start with a mantra. A mantra is usually short: a syllable, word, or phrase that you repeat. Some people of faith will choose a very short verse from scripture.

While a meditation mantra is rooted in Buddhism and Hinduism, Judeo-Christian meditation practices are also a spiritual tradition. In this tradition, they will use sacred words like "Abba" or "Peace" as the mantra. Some Christians will use "breath prayers" as their mantra, inhaling with a focus on the name of their creator, then exhaling the word they want to expel or lift up to God.

Your mantra can be anything you choose. I find it helpful to consider what it is I long for in that moment: Peace? Comfort? Calmness?

Is there a word, a phrase, or a name that will provide that for you? An uttering? A sound? I'll invite you to adopt a mantra that is helpful to you. As you meditate, you will speak it aloud, chant, whisper, or even repeat silently in your mind.

Select a mantra that focuses your longings and stay with it. Breathe slowly. Attend to your senses as a way of releasing tension. When your mind wanders—and it will—gently refocus on your mantra.

At first, your attention will drift a lot. Set a timer, and you'll notice your first meditation lasts for 30 seconds. Tomorrow you may last one minute. The next day, two minutes; the next day, three minutes; and so on. Perfection is not the goal. The only goal is your practice. This is a meditation practice.

The benefits of meditation for mental health are clear. According to the Mayo Clinic, "Meditation can give you a sense of calm, peace and balance that can benefit both your emotional well-being and your overall health." Meditation aids in relaxation, stress management, reduced anxiety, and emotional regulation.

I'm only asking you to try it for thirty seconds to start.

Flow

Mihaly Csikszentmihalyi (pronounced "Me-high Chick-sent-me-high-ee") is a positive psychologist who developed a theory called "flow."

You've experienced it. I know you have. Remember when you were so immersed in a task that everything around you faded away? You were so absorbed in it, you felt hyper focused?

Time stood still. You didn't feel hungry. You didn't need the restroom (or couldn't be bothered to go).

You were challenged near the top of your ability, but you were also competent enough in the task to solve the problems that came up. You could identify the next thing that needed to happen without thinking too hard about it. Quitting didn't occur to you.

Athletes call it "the zone." Others call it the "sweet spot." For me, it's getting lost in my pottery.

When have you felt flow? What were you doing? What was it like? How can you return to it?

First, carve out time for it. It's hard to find flow in five-minute increments. Give yourself at least an hour. More, if you are able.

Then, clear your mind of worry. Decide not to think about work, emails, family, or tasks while you're engaging in your flow task. I schedule my worry. I literally put it in my phone's calendar: "Monday morning at 10:30: worry about finances, search for a new accounting software."

If you have it on your calendar, then it won't bother you when you are engaging in your flow activity. You can remove the mental clutter.

You might also need to remove the physical clutter. Right now my pottery studio is in my laundry room. This means I have to move all the clean laundry out and throw the dirty stuff in the washer. But this act of clearing out my space helps my mind prepare for the activity I get to engage in. It's almost Pavlovian.

To get into a state of flow, and to eliminate distractions, get your resources together. If you are going to bake, gather your ingredients and your materials, the mixer, the bowls, baking pans, measuring cups and spoons.

For me, I need a clean work surface, the slab roller, canvas, cutting tools, pottery wheel, water, slip.

For my husband, who plays a concert grand electro-acoustic harp for fun, he needs to get his glass of wine, his music, the amps turned on, other sounds turned off, and the cat out of the room.

Finally, grab a water bottle, maybe have a snack handy, use the rest room, and then set a timer if you need to.

As you are moving through this routine of preparation, you are also thinking about where to start. Planning what you want to accomplish.

Flow is the full immersion in an activity. It focuses on the task, the external process. Presence focuses on the internal processes.

Both are a form of mindfulness.

Gratitude

I have a friend who started a habit of a daily Facebook post of one thing she was grateful for. Her rule was that she couldn't list the same thing twice. I can't recall the exact number, but she was on a 1000+ day streak last I read. Do you know how joyful this woman is? I am pretty sure she wasn't nearly this happy before she started.

Gratitude is the little sister to mindfulness. Mindful people fully immerse themselves in activities, and they often notice the positive experiences of life. And they tend to be grateful.

In essence, they savor the good experiences.

In my Positive Psychology class, I assign my students several tasks: Notice beauty. Create a meditation practice for a week. Savor a raisin.

On the first day of class, they are given five minutes to list all the things in their life that have gone right. "I have a bed." "I was born alive." "I am able to see." At the end of the five minutes, they have very long lists.

Later in the same class period, I ask them, "As you lay your head on your pillow, what needs to have happened that day for you to say, 'Today was a good day?'" So many will say, "laughter," "time with friends," or "playing with my dog."

How would you answer the questions?

I also give my students an assignment on gratitude.

I ask them to follow these three steps: every day, look for good things. Witness kindness. Observe happy moments. Bear witness to someone else's resilience. Notice your own.

The first step in all these exercises is that you start paying attention to something good. Gratitude is no different.

Have you ever walked into a place and scanned for the bad? You look for the ugly, the damaged, the broken or unkempt? Maybe you scan your loved ones for what is wrong with them instead of what is right? It is so hard to be grateful when you are looking for something to complain about.

The first facet of gratitude is shifting your focus onto what is lovely. Notice beauty around you.

But after you notice it, you have to really pay attention to it; absorb the moment. What is it that makes it beautiful? I am inviting you to savor it.

In their gratitude reflections, students write: "This person just offered to take my cart so I didn't have to push it back to the cart corral." "The sunset isn't just pink. It has blue, purple, magenta, and orange and yellow down by the horizon." "Someone complimented me on my shirt. I didn't think it was special, but she did. And she took the time to tell me!"

Notice it; savor it. And then, express it.

Thank someone; acknowledge gratitude to yourself. For it to become a practice, journal it. It becomes permanent when you record it.

You don't have to write it, although that is the traditional method. You can speak it into a voice memo, using your mic on your notes app. Send it to yourself in a text each night.

You can even tell someone else at the end of the day. While everyone dishes up their dinner, make them say three things (that haven't already been said) that they are grateful for before you give them their silverware.

They're gonna love that.

The assignment for the students was to journal three things they were grateful for every day. While they had to do this for academic credit, it also helped them adjust their focus and their attitude.

At the start of the semester, one student listed,

1. I'm grateful for fizzy water in the cafeteria.
2. I'm grateful for Amazon shopping.
3. I'm grateful for my boyfriend.

By the end of the semester the same student wrote,

- I'm grateful I had a flat tire today.
- My grandpa died last year, but when I was in middle school, he taught me how to change a tire. He made me practice on his pickup. I'm grateful he did that. I wasn't grateful at the time. I thought he was just mean.
- I'm grateful I remembered what he taught me. That I knew how to do this on my own. I was more capable than I thought I was.
- I'm also grateful I had the stuff I needed in my trunk. I was surprised there was a spare tire and a jack in there. I had no idea!
- I'm grateful that so many people actually stopped to help me even though I didn't really need them to. It was morning rush-hour traffic and three different people stopped!
- And I am grateful I had a flat tire because it let me miss my 8 am Chemistry class.

Knowing that you will be recording your gratitude each evening forces you to be more aware of good things throughout the day.

Whatever is true, whatever is lovely, whatever is admirable, or beautiful, pay attention to these things. Gratitude brings you peace.

Finally, I assign these students to write a gratitude letter. They compose a physical letter to someone in their life who had a positive impact or did a kind thing for them. Usually, it is something that the student has remembered for more than a year. It is a lingering gratitude.

I invite them to connect with that person and read the letter aloud to them, face-to-face, virtually, or by phone. If the person is no longer around, they can read it aloud to the gravestone, the urn, an empty chair, etc.

Then, to finish the assignment, the student reflects on the experience. In course evaluations, some students say the gratitude letter was the most moving assignment of the semester.

Gratitude = 1) notice, 2) savor or appreciate, 3) record. These three steps will change your focus. They will change your attitude. They may transform you.

There are myriad research studies that show mindfulness, savoring, and gratitude all enhance life satisfaction. Science gives us evidence that you will love your life more if you engage in these three practices.

If this is something that appeals to you, I invite you to do any of the following. Set a timer to call yourself to awareness throughout the day. Start your day with morning pages. What is your mantra? Download a meditation app on your phone. Develop a spiritual discipline or devotion time. Start a gratitude journal.

Savoring, meditation, flow, or gratitude: if you develop any one of these as a practice, you will be astounded at the positive changes to your mental health.

Moving forward, as you begin each new chapter, I invite you to create a state of mindfulness, to enter into a flow state, to savor the words as they move your emotions, and to answer your questions with an ear towards gratitude.

Application

Now pause reading for a minute. Take a deep breath. Eliminate distractions. Put on some peaceful background music.

- In what ways do you linger in the past?
- What are the consequences of that?
- When do you over-focus on the future?
- What are the consequences of that?
- When are you fully present, completely focused, living in the moment?
- What does that feel like for you?

Emotional Awareness

Using the vocabulary of emotions, close your eyes and point to a word in the strong category, preferably from depression to remorse. Imagine feeling that emotion right now.

- Where is it located in the body?
- Where does tension reside?
- Is there physical pain? Numbness? Heaviness?

Repeat the exercise with another word selected from a different category.

Unfinished business
This might feel slightly uncomfortable, but it might also be helpful for you.

Looking at the vocabulary of emotions, what are the emotions most common to you?

- Choose one and bring it to mind. Does it remind you of an event?
- What happened that feels unresolved to you in this moment? Your answer may be different the next time you do this exercise.
- When you are moving through the next 24 hours, and you feel a strong emotion, pause and ask yourself, "What was I just thinking about?"
- Does this emotion feel tied to a situation that has not been fully processed?
- Are there pieces of the event that feel unresolved?
- Are there physical experiences or behavior components that signal unfinished business for you?

"It" vs. "I" and "I" vs. "They"
- When do you tend to use the word "it?" What are the specific statements that follow the word "it"? How can you change these statements to "I?"
- When have you given in to the tyranny of "they"? What are the statements you tend to use that credit "they" for your pressures, stress, or indecision?

- Once you have isolated one of these moments, ask yourself,
- Who are "they"? Why do I let them matter so much?
- What do I want instead?
- What do I need in my life?
- What will nourish me?

Savoring

Select a small, bite sized morsel and use the following prompts to savor it:

Sight: examine the item and describe what you see. Look at the color, texture, shape. What else do you notice?

Touch: feel the texture, temperature, firmness, softness. Explore it with your fingers. How would you describe the feel of it?

Smell: hold it close to your nose and inhale slowly. What does it smell like? Can you think of five different words to describe the smell?

Taste: Now, put it in your mouth and roll it around. What do you notice before you bite into it? Choose five words to label those sensations.

As you bite down on it gently, what happens? What five flavors can you isolate?

Sound: Listen to the sound of your chewing. What words can you use to describe the sound?

Interoception: Notice the sensations as you swallow. What words would you use to describe that internal transition from teeth to tongue to throat to stomach?

MORNINGS

- Describe your usual morning routine.
- Each morning, is there some way you can create before you consume?
- Will you consider trying morning pages for three mornings? To do this, you will need at least nine empty pages. Remind yourself this is a brain dump and not to be judged or edited. Nobody is allowed to read it. Not even you.
- Write in long-hand, whatever comes to mind—no correcting, no editing, no judgment. When you have reached three pages, stop.
- Repeat this tomorrow. And the next morning.
    - What do you notice about how your day feels after doing this exercise?
    - Is this a practice you can schedule each morning? It doesn't take long and can be done while hiding in the bathroom.

Meditation

To select a mantra, is there a word that aligns with a longing or a need? Go back in this chapter to locate the relaxation technique. When you have found it, set your timer and settle into your meditation. There are also good meditation apps on your phone.

How might you aside an extra 15 minutes each morning before your day starts to develop a spiritual discipline or devotion time?

Could you set aside an extra five minutes at the end of your day to record the beauty you saw in a gratitude journal?

4
PLOT
How am I telling my story?

Sunday mornings were always chaos. Growing up, we attended church religiously.

I was sitting in my highchair—I don't know how old I was. There were eight kids in the family. The youngest sat in the highchair and slept in the crib until the next baby came along.

There was a flurry of activity around me. My brothers rough-housing. My mother yelling, "BOYS!" My dad starting the car.

I watched each person racing out, the screen door slamming behind them. I watched them through the window where I was sitting in my highchair. They all piled into the station wagon.

Of course, my mother was last to run out the door. I watched her get in the car. I heard the *thunk'* of her car door shutting. I watched the car back away from the house. It drove away from the yard. It crunched the gravel as it headed down the driveway.

They forgot me.

That's my story.

When I reminded my mother of that memory when I was a teen, she dismissed it: "Ach! That never happened."

Of course she wouldn't remember it. They caught themselves before they turned onto the road. My dad put the car in reverse and backed up the driveway. He pulled in front of the house. My mother ran in and released me from my highchair. Lifted me out, tucked me under her arm. Off to church we went.

No. She didn't recall it. For her, it was less than 30 seconds of her life. For me, it was life-defining.

My other early memory was of me climbing out of my crib around age three. I was supposed to be napping. I don't remember anything more. Half a century later, at a recent family gathering, a brother commented on the story. He still remembers when it happened.

I don't know who noticed I was gone. They couldn't find me anywhere. Everybody searched: my older brothers, my sister, my parents.

My dad said the first thing he did was check the hog barn (sows can be lethal omnivores). He was so worried I had gotten too close to the hog pen and they had torn me apart.

Next, he searched the cow tank. It was a large, open tank of water, taller than I was at that time. It was continuously fed from an underground well so that it was always full, keeping the cows hydrated year-round. My dad worried I had fallen in somehow and had drowned.

My family searched everywhere. My parents were in a panic. They didn't know how or why I had vanished. What if I had wandered down the road? Being so small, might I have been hard to see and hit by a car? Was I lying broken and bloodied in the tall grasses of a ditch? What if I was lost in the woods and couldn't find my way home? They even worried I'd been abducted before child abductions were a common concern.

They continued to search for what felt like hours, my dad later told me. He said he had never been so scared in his whole life.

He said they wept with relief when our neighbor, Mr. Peterson, walked me up the driveway and back to my parents' empty arms.

Apparently, I'd spent the afternoon watching him work on his tractor. He said I had wandered over there to see if he had any donuts.

Alfred Adler

Alfred Adler held that our earliest memories tell us how to view our lives and ourselves. Your early memories can identify themes in your personality. Your memories can give reasons to behaviors you don't understand on a conscious level.

I find this theory interesting in light of my two earliest memories.

Except—are they real memories?

Most memories are flawed. Your memories are inexact, blurry, changed with time. You add in new information, and you subtract other information. Memories are almost always inaccurate.

Did either of those stories happen exactly as I told them to you? Unlikely.

And yet, I tell these stories to other people just like I told them here. When I talk about Adler's theories in my Principles of Counseling class, I tell my students these two early memories.

I tell these stories to my students in my Introduction to Psychology class when we discuss the inaccuracy of memory.

I tell these two stories to my children when I want a cute little anecdote about growing up on the farm with so many siblings. When we visit the swine barn at the fair, I tell them the story of how my dad thought I'd been eaten by a pig.

I especially tell these two stories to myself whenever I feel forgotten, unseen, or alone. I've let these two stories become life themes for me.

I remind myself that I am overlooked. I am easily lost. I am isolated. I am forgettable.

Narrative therapy

Narrative therapy holds that much of your life is viewed through stories. Some stories stand out to you as more significant. Others are never told once you have lived them.

In class the other day, I taught my students a group therapy exercise called "lifeline." Group members are each given a piece of paper and a pencil. They draw a line across the paper with peaks and valleys and plateaus reflecting the significant moments in their lives. Each significant dip and peak is labeled with a word. Then they show the rest of the group the line. They point out the high and low points, reading the words to the group: graduation, marriage, job loss, baby, depression, divorce.

It is hard to do because we have stories about those events that we really want to tell! The whole point of the exercise is to quickly and efficiently give information about oneself without the clutter of long stories.

You tell your stories all the time. When you leave work at the end of the day, a colleague asks, "How was your day?" and you answer with a story. When your doctor asks you, "What brings you in?" you tell them a story of your symptoms and how they are affecting you. You chat with a neighbor during the backyard barbecue, and you tell them a story about your roof.

We connect with others through story. I tell you about the death of my husband, and you tell me about losing your grandma. You tell me a story of your teenager struggling, and I'll tell you a story about mine.

Your business is looking at more budget cuts? Mine too! You have a bunch of stories about how your kids drive you crazy?

Yeah. Me too.

Coffee shops are filled with people sharing their stories. Homes burst with stories that are being written. And my clients come in with baskets overflowing with stories.

But, you see, many of these stories are problem saturated.

I have a client who just got engaged a few months ago. That is such good news, but the stories she shares are challenges of planning the wedding. The stories are all about the problems.

My friend has the cutest set of infant twins. The stories of her sleepless nights are exhausting to hear though. As an empath, every time I see her, I crave a nap.

You get the idea. You connect with others, usually through your shared stories, and those stories usually focus on hassles, hardships, or pain.

Why is that bad?

It isn't. They become a problem when they become your *only* stories, and particularly when they become the only stories you tell yourself. You tell me stories that say, "My partner never tells me they love me." But are you disregarding all the things they do to demonstrate their love?

Your story is "My boss is always cranky with me." But you are not telling the rest of the story. Your boss is parenting a difficult teen, they are putting their mom in assisted living, and their partner is emotionally absent. Of course they are cranky. It's not about you at all.

Problem-Saturated Stories

These problem-saturated stories pose a risk to your mental health when they start to define you. When they define the other people in your life. When they define your life.

Your stories, especially the stories you tell yourself, shape your reality. They create what you see, how you feel, where you go, and what you do.

If a main story is that you struggled in school, your stories around that struggle may create a broad story of failure. Of stupidity. Of insecurity.

If you repeatedly tell yourself the story of being bullied, your life story becomes one of chronic victimization.

While these stories are true, the problem happens when they are the only stories you tell yourself.

Sometimes you adopt your stories from what others have told you. My story about wandering off was a story my dad told. It became *my* memory.

Here is what I find interesting. Dad said I went to the neighbor's house looking for a donut. This was his punchline.

But his punchline became my life theme. When I was morbidly obese, I used one tiny snippet of his story of me to inform my gluttonous behaviors. His punchline explained my binge-eating disorder. It defined my struggle with food.

I ignored the part about my family searching everywhere. My mother's panic. The terror my dad felt looking for my little body, fearing he might find me dead.

My dad told a story of deep love, of frantic searching, of overwhelming relief! He never intended the "looking for a do-nut" part to be anything but a cute anecdote to lighten the story, but I made it a core truth of my identity.

Do you do this? Do you tell your stories as a way of high-lighting your pain? Your struggle? Your failures or incompeten-cies? If you do, you are not alone. It has become a national pas-time: sharing our hard stories.

But what are you leaving out? What is the part of the story that speaks to a greater truth about you? Where is the positive spin?

The first question I ask myself when I am with a client is "What are the stories they are telling?" Usually, the stories that come up in therapy are extremely painful. They are indicative of the struggle that brought them in for help in the first place. And that is a great place to start.

Externalizing the Problem

One of my favorite podcasts is "The Hilarious World of Depres-sion" with John Moe. It's no longer being recorded. I remember exactly where I was when I heard him announce he was going to stop.

Occasionally John Moe featured call-ins where people could record their story on the podcast's voicemail. One young woman called in from Minnesota and told her story about her experience at the Mall of America (MoA).

As an aside, MoA is huge: four stories high, with a complete Nickelodeon-themed indoor amusement park. There are multiple open rotundas throughout the mall. From the top floor, you can look over the railing and watch the concerts happening on the bottom floor.

I can't find the episode anymore. I'll paraphrase the story in my own words and in the first person. Forgive me, reader, if it was you who called this in and I completely botch your story.

I go shopping with friends once in a while at the Mall of America. Every time I walk in there, an intrusive thought tells me to go to the fourth floor and jump off the rotunda. This intrusive thought keeps trying to make me kill myself!

I talked about it with my therapist.

He told me to give the voice a name. He said the problem wasn't me. The voice had an agenda. It was trying to ruin my fun at the mall. I didn't want to waste my time there being terrified I might kill myself in front of a bunch of people. I just wanted to go shopping and get some ice cream with my friends. I didn't want to kill myself. The problem wasn't me.

So I named the problem "Steve."

Next time I went to the mall with my friends, Steve told me to jump off the fourth floor into the rotunda. Like always, he was really insistent.

But I stopped. Right there in the middle of the mall. I stopped walking. Out loud I said, "Steve, that is the dumbest idea I have ever heard. You need to shut up."

And he did! I mean, I had to tell him that a bunch of times, but Steve finally went away when I went to the mall.

Isn't that a great story? One of the goals of narrative therapy is to help you externalize the problem so you aren't the problem.

Do you internalize the problem so it becomes a character flaw, a failure, and identity? Are you making the punchline of someone else's story into your own personal struggle? Are you making the mean voices in your head become an internal dialogue that you have allowed to describe you?

Plot

When I started writing this book, my writing coach gave me some instructions before I even began the first page. He said, "Create a brief statement of what you want to convey, and create an outline that will help you convey it."

You are the author of your life. You are writing a book in your head whenever you think about your life. It's just not intentionally written.

But you can be more intentional about it. If you were to write about where you started and where you hope to end, what would be your outline?

Look back at the title of this chapter: it's called "Plot." Narrative therapy invites you to look for the themes that emerge when you tell your stories.

What is a common problem that comes to mind for you right now? Can you map the effects this problem has on you?

When you think of your life in narrative terms, this problem is the conflict of the story.

When I was little, I watched the *Bob Newhart Show* on Saturday nights. He was a psychologist in Chicago. He had an office full of funny patients. He lived in a condo overlooking the city.

I wanted to be a psychologist. That is all I wanted to be when I grew up. Nothing else. I was going to be Bob Newhart.

Sitting in front of my guidance counselor in high school, as we tried to plan out my future, I told him my big dream of being a psychologist.

He looked at my miserable grades, shrugged and shook his head. Without making eye contact he said, "Maybe we should take a different track."

He slid something from a local vocational school across the desk to me. It was a brochure for a meat-cutting program. Apparently, when he looked at me, he saw the word *Butcher.*

I get queasy handling chicken cutlets. I can't eat bone-in wings because the bones make me feel lightheaded. I lose my appetite if I have to trim the fat off a prime rib. A rare steak feels too…honest.

I have nothing against meat-cutters. I am grateful they exist. They hold an important role in our society. But there was no way I could be one!

The problem wasn't the actual event. The guidance counselor telling me to become a butcher was not the issue.

The problem was the way I told myself that story.

I convinced myself the guidance counselor didn't think I had what it took to become a psychologist. He did not think I was smart enough for university work. I was not capable of continuing my education. He doubted my potential.

My story was this: "I am not enough."

So I didn't go to college after high school.

I didn't go to college for years. I left out a lot of information when I told myself that story, and the missing information completely derailed my life.

What about your problematic story? Do you have a story that derails you? The story that stops you in your tracks? What is the story that keeps you from even trying? If you aren't sure, can you ask someone who might see you more clearly than you see yourself?

Conflict

As you write the story, you define the conflict.

Consider how the problem has been disruptive, dominating, or discouraging. What is the agenda of this problem, and how has it been winning? What power are you giving it?

But every author, after identifying the conflict, examines possible outcomes. You search for false solutions, attempts that failed.

Then you find the true solution.

If the conflict is loneliness, the outcome would be love. If the conflict is loss, the conclusion is redemption. If the conflict is victimization, the solution is victory.

Do you see where I am going with this?

The problem you are struggling with is the conflict. So what's the solution? You may already have the solution or have lived the solution.

In your story that you are living, you are the antagonist. In this story of your life, the main character is you. I hope you are writing yourself as a hero.

Look at your story again. How can you tell the story differently?

This is the goal of narrative therapy.

The Rest of the Story

Did I really wander off to get a donut?

Everyone in my house was paired up. Birth order theory would say I was an only child in this sea of children. Ran and Jeff were close in age and the best of friends. Mike and Dave were practically the same person. Brad and Brenda were allies when they weren't enemies. My parents had eyes only for each other. I was the odd one out. I didn't have anyone close to my age; I didn't have a best friend in the house. I usually felt alone.

But Mr. Peterson? He was so kind, always happy to see me. He was easy to be around. I wanted to hang out with him.

By telling the story differently to myself, I am not the chubby kid just wanting a donut. I was a lonely little girl looking for connection and choosing a good solution.

What parts of the story have you left out? What alternative meanings exist?

Sometimes you tell a story as though it is the full truth and there are no exceptions to it. But you actually leave a critical piece of information out.

When I tell the story about my guidance counselor telling me to become a butcher, I leave out a huge piece of information.

My grades *were* abysmal. I graduated high school *summa per dentes meos*" (Latin for "by the skin of my teeth").

From the time I was in kindergarten, teacher comments on my report cards routinely read, "Mitzi talks too much in class," "I have to keep moving her to get her to stop interrupting her neighbors," "Mitzi is very disruptive," "She is a daydreamer," "Mitzi doesn't pay attention to instructions."

In the student teacher conferences, they would say, "You are missing 15 of the 21 assignments in math that are due up to this point." To my mother, they would say, "Your daughter is not working up to her full potential."

All of these comments pointed to my personal failure as a student. I was a chatty nuisance. I was lazy. My teachers didn't think I was taking school seriously. I just wasn't trying hard enough.

Later, as a psychologist who conducted neuropsychological assessments for both a local medical school and the Minneapolis Public Schools, I understand that those comments reflected clear indications of my undiagnosed, untreated Attention Deficit Disorder. I had a classic case of it. But as a girl in a small school in the 1980s, I never received a diagnosis. Therefore, I didn't get any help.

But now that I know that I have ADD, I am so relieved! When I tell my story of undiagnosed ADD, I give my younger self some grace. My poor grades weren't a personal failure. I wasn't lazy. I didn't lack motivation.

Including this information in my story finally gave me answers. It made sense why it felt like I was working so much harder than everyone else and still not keeping up. I can see my struggle was not a flaw. It was neurodiversity unrecognized.

But my early theme of the story was failure. I was a stupid, unmotivated person who would never go to college. I couldn't be a psychologist because I was dumb. I couldn't be a butcher because I fainted at the sight of raw meat.

The way I told my story almost ruined me.

I ended up moving to Los Angeles to become an actress. A series of hard events caused me to become homeless, facing down some awful choices. But I believed I deserved to be in this situation.

It was my fault because I hadn't tried harder in school, and I wasn't smart enough to succeed. My story was that I had become an abject failure.

I guess some would call it serendipity that the driver of a large truck wasn't paying attention and slammed into the back of my car, which was also my home. The car was totaled, and his insurance paid out just enough money to cover the value of the car. It wasn't much but it was enough to get me back to my midwestern roots.

Back to your story, the one you are telling yourself: what parts of the story have you left out? What alternative meanings exist?

And how would someone else tell your story to you? If someone else was also there, how would they tell the story? If someone else really knows and loves you, how do they tell your story differently?

There are people around you who have a very different version from yours. And usually, when you put the two stories together, theirs and yours, you get a more accurate version of the truth.

After moving back to the upper Midwest, I visited my sister. She lived near a university campus in North Dakota.

One day the weather was mild, and she suggested we walk over and enjoy the beauty of the campus. It was the middle of the week, and offices were open.

Once there, she suggested we wander through the buildings. We ended up in the admissions office. She asked the nice lady behind the desk what it would take for me to go to school there.

I wanted to refuse the conversation. I had a hard story, and I had committed to a hard life.

But my sister saw my story differently. She knew a story of resilience. I had survived homelessness in the San Fernando Valley and lived to talk about it. My sister held a story of a bright, courageous sister who held potential.

As she asked the admissions counselor how to get me into their program, my sister told me the hopeful story of me going to college, of chasing my dream, making a plan, having a different life. She told me the story of me as a future psychologist.

Your Story

How are you telling your stories? What are the good parts you are omitting? What are alternative explanations? When were you not dominated or discouraged by the problem? What evidence is there to bolster a new way of telling it?

Open yourself up in the way you answer these questions. You have stood up to the problem in the past. You have proven to yourself that it isn't the WHOLE story. You have escaped the dominance of the problem at times.

What are the exceptions? What have you overcome already? Where have you grown in the face of hardships?

Let's take a minute to look back at how you answered questions from previous chapters: what gives your life purpose? What do you want? What do you need? What gives your life passion? Where do you have fun?

Now, answer this: how have your stories gotten in the way of meeting your purpose? Your values? Your wants and needs? Your passion? Your playfulness?

What stories have you left out and not told yourself?

What are the stories that point to your potential?

I finally listened to my sister tell her story of me. I went to college. I worked full time and studied full time. I majored in Psychology, Philosophy, and World Religions. I was on the dean's list every semester.

I earned the highest rank of *Summa Cum Laude* and was accepted into a graduate program with my first application.

Now I have my master's in clinical psychology and a doctorate in clinical and forensic psychology. I am a tenured professor and the former chair of a department of psychology. I teach in both undergraduate and graduate programs. I sit on dissertation committees. I see patients; I coach clients. I am an international consultant on subjects of mental health. I speak at conferences, conventions, and corporations all over the world.

A butcher?

Eat it, Mr. Muchlinski.

I invite you to rewrite your story. Tell the whole truth, including your resilience, your strengths, your successes and victories.

You have way more potential than you tell yourself.

Just ask my sister.

Application

Take a break from your reading. Inhale and exhale slowly a couple times. Now, think about the stories you have been telling lately.

- What are the most common stories you tell?
- How are you telling these stories?
- What are the good parts you are omitting?
- What are alternative explanations?
- When were you not dominated or discouraged by the problem?
- What evidence is there to bolster a new way of telling it?
- What are the exceptions?
- What have you overcome already?
- Where have you grown in the face of hardships?

- How have your stories (or how you've told them) gotten in your way? Of fulfilling your purpose? Of following your passion?
- How have your stories blocked you from meeting your needs?
- How can you rewrite one of these stories to point to your potential?
- How can you make yourself the hero of your past stories?
- How can you make yourself the hero of the next story you write?

5
PERSPECTIVE
What am I saying to myself?

Cognitive Theory

Josie has two PhDs. She is a scientist in a top-tier organization. She dresses impeccably, speaks articulately. Her posture is erect, hair straight and smooth, and her shoes are polished and pristine.

At the start of one of our first sessions, as we were sitting down and getting comfortable, I asked, "How's your day going?"

She told me the story of not being able to find the camisole that goes with the suit she had on. She couldn't find it anywhere. She emptied every drawer, pulled down every hanger, dumped out all the laundry. She stripped all the bedding off the bed. She couldn't find it.

A frustrating story. Her method of trying to find it showed diligence and, albeit messy, resolve.

Then she admitted that, as she searched, she called herself vile names. She used words that made me blush. She favored a word that started with "F" and ended in "king," followed by a word that starts with "R" and ends in "tard."

I will be frank in telling you I find the first word unbearably common and the second one simply offensive.

Stringing those two together was Josie's phrase to describe herself in her own head.

I asked her if this phrase was a common reaction to something like misplacing a camisole.

Without apology or excuse, she said, "I say this all day. Every day. It's who I am."

This is a woman with two PhDs.

Cognitive Therapy

Cognitive Therapy was developed by Aaron Beck as an evidence-based therapy for the treatment of depression. He used a lot of research to support this theory.

He believed much of our distress is an exaggeration of normal functioning. Josie was searching for an item of clothing. Normal functioning.

But her emotional reaction was extreme: she called herself awful things. She dumped all her items out onto the floor in anger at herself. She knew she would be going home to every piece of clothing she owned, and all her bedding, in a mountain on the floor.

Do you exaggerate responses to things, people, events in your own life? What are some of your extreme reactions? Do you have emotional outbursts? Harsh criticisms of yourself or others? Are you sobbing? Shutting down? Procrastinating? Getting stuck and avoiding your impossible tasks?

Beck's theory holds that how you *think* influences how you *feel*. Those feelings then inform how you *act*.

When you have a distorted perspective, your emotions and your behaviors will become distorted too. For Josie, her thoughts about herself caused extreme hostility that caused her to dump her clothes on the floor. How she thought influenced how she felt, and that affected her behavior.

It all started with her thoughts.

Cognitive distortions

Cognitive distortions are skewed ways of thinking. Here are a few examples:

Josie shared with me that she is pretty sure her boss is going to fire her eventually. Josie just isn't as smart as everyone else on her team.

What's she basing that on? What's her evidence? She doesn't have any proof that she will get fired. She is just sure it's going to happen. This is an "arbitrary inference."

Arbitrary inferences

Arbitrary inferences are conclusions you draw without evidence. "I'm going to get a flat tire on my way to work. I just know it." But your tires are new, and the roads on your commute are good.

When you walk into a room of people, you think, "Everyone can tell I am a loser." That is an arbitrary inference. There is no factual evidence to support what they think. In fact, the evidence would be that people probably aren't really thinking about you at all. Most of us are too self-involved to notice.

Selective abstraction

Sometimes you get upset when you engage in "selective abstraction." You make assumptions or develop beliefs about something based on an isolated event. You let one incident ruin you.

I walked around the back of the room during a lecture one time and saw a student on Zappos. I was talking about a criminal defense called Not Guilty by Reason of Insanity (NGRI), and she was shopping for shoes!

This incident has permanently convinced me that I am boring. I am positive that, if students' laptops are open, they are doing something more interesting than listening to me drone on about the criminal justice system or psychological theories.

But I hold on to that weird belief that everyone is bored based on one isolated event with one student. Do you know how many other times I've seen student laptops open? How often have I wandered around the classroom and saw they aren't shopping for shoes? Most of the time! They are looking at my slide deck for the lecture, they are on the class webpage, or they are taking notes. These are the common themes I see on their laptops.

And yet, I continue to assume the students are not paying attention. I let my feelings be hurt, based on that one student experience. Selective abstraction.

When have you made yourself feel bad because of one event? Do you continue to focus on that event, even in the face of a lot of contrary evidence? Have you walked into a party and noticed an awkward look directed your way? When you got home, did you fixate on that, try to make sense of it? Did you dismiss the many smiles you got the whole time you were there?

Also, let's be honest about the laptop thing. If I was still in college and had a laptop in class, I'd be on Zappos too. I have ADD, and I love shoes. My search for the perfect espadrille would not be a reflection on the quality of the professor's teaching.

Overgeneralization

Overgeneralization is similar to arbitrary abstraction. Arbitrary abstraction is applying a single example as evidence across the board. Overgeneralization is applying that one incident as evidence about something else entirely.

Let's say you were let go from a job as part of a budgetary decision at your company. You were one of many who were affected during this layoff.

You take it personally and decide that you will never find another job. Because you are sure that you are trash, you will never find love, either. Nobody can love a loser that can't hold down a job.

Overgeneralization happens when we hold an extreme belief about an event or idea. Then we take that belief and apply it to other situations that aren't even like the original. You used your thoughts about the layoff to destroy your hopes for a relationship.

Have you overgeneralized? Do you make huge assumptions about yourself (or others) based on a single piece of information?

Magnification and Minimization

Seeing a situation as much bigger or much smaller than it deserves to be is called magnification and minimization.

I request feedback from speaking engagements. I especially appreciate audience comments from the post-event surveys.

Okay, "appreciate" is not the right word. I especially "ignore all the nice things people say and I overvalue negative audience comments from the post-event surveys."

There will be 400 positive comments: "She was so funny!" "I loved her content!" "I've already started applying her suggestions." "She was amazing!" "I loved her shoes!"

Wow. So nice.

But then I see one hard comment, "I thought she would speak more about humor." Immediately I want to ball up the entire 20 pages of comments and throw them in the fireplace.

I ruminate about that one comment. I feel so ashamed. I decide I will never speak again. I am a terrible speaker. I don't deserve to be onstage.

I magnified the importance of one critical comment. I minimized the comments from the audience that were affirming.

What do you magnify? Your deficits? Your flaws? Do you magnify how you hurt someone else? Do you fixate on that one thing you said that one time?

And what do you minimize? Compliments? The kindnesses you've shown to others? Your adorable presence? Your irresistible charm? Your skills? Your talents? Your resilience?

Personalization

Personalization is another distorted way of thinking. It happens when you assume responsibility for something that is completely outside your control. You are not responsible, but you still take the blame.

When I found out I couldn't be a psychologist, I moved out to Los Angeles and became an actress. I quickly found work with a repertory theater company.

I traveled around the US performing in schools, prisons, churches, military bases, etc.

It was okay. I didn't love it. It was something to kill time while trying to figure out how *not* to become a butcher.

One of the plays we performed focused on suicide prevention, and I played the lead. During a performance at a high school, I messed up one of the lines. It wasn't a terrible mistake; I transposed a few words from the script. I hadn't changed the plot or meaning of the play, but I was still mad at myself.

A few days later our troupe learned that a student at that school had died by suicide. I convinced myself it was because I had messed up the lines. I had (in my head) killed this kid.

I was a wreck. I was heartbroken.

And I was wrong.

This was an extreme case of personalization. I believed I was responsible for this young man's death, even though I was not involved in the situation at all. I was in no way connected to the event. I was not even adjacent to it.

What do you personalize? What are you taking on as your responsibility? What do you think you control when it's got nothing at all to do with you? What are you owning that you do not own?

Labeling
Sometimes you fixate on your imperfections. You occupy your mind with mistakes that you have made. Then you label them in such a way that they inform who you think you are. You assume them as your identity.

Let's look at Josie, my double-doctorate client. She labeled herself so cruelly. She used the words, "f--king r-tard" as a personal label. These words are so offensive, so damaging. They made her believe she didn't deserve her degrees, her job, or her title.

How are you labeling yourself? Are there words you favor to insult yourself? Do you label your past mistakes or current imperfections? Have these labels become your identity?

Say aloud the first word(s) that come to mind when you finish this sentence: "I am (a) _____."

Is that word is an insult?

But is it fair? Is it accurate? Is it hurtful?

Sometimes I will ask a client, "Would you label someone you loved with this word? Or your best friend? Your grandma?"

If not, it's probably a mislabel. It is likely inaccurate and unfair.

Dichotomous Thinking

Finally, Beck theorized that you may have distorted thoughts that are dichotomous. Do you use either-or statements? Either you are perfect, or you are a loser. Either you succeed all the time, or you are a failure.

You are always a good student, or you are flunking. Everything works out for you, or nothing works out for you. They never help out around the house. They always try to control you.

Do you see the language just used? Either-or? Always-Never? Everything-Nothing? Success-Failure? Perfect-Loser? These are dichotomies. They are black and white.

But you live your life in the grey. Very rarely is something always this or never that. No one is a perfect success or a perfect failure. The grey area allows for mistakes, for ambiguity, for tolerance of flaws, even permission.

Chet was a CEO of a large corporation. His marriage was good; his kids were healthy. He liked his friends. He loved to golf.

But a major depressive episode hit him in his early forties, and it set out to destroy him. It became so painful, he quit his very important job.

He sunk lower and lower, convinced he was a failure. He tried to golf one day but made it through two holes before he gave up and went home. He didn't golf again that year.

His symptoms were so bad, he prayed at night that he wouldn't wake up. His wife finally said, "You need to get help, or you need to get out."

This didn't surprise him. Chet knew it was bad. He needed to do something, so he went on an antidepressant. He started exercising half an hour every morning. And he went to therapy.

The therapist said, "You keep telling me that you are a failure. I want you to go home tonight and make a list of all the things you've failed at."

Chet started the list. He thought he'd fill pages. He wrote down two items and then he got stuck. He couldn't recall any more than that.

He had developed dichotomous thinking. He believed if he quit his important job, he must be an utter failure.

But when making the list, he only had a couple instances. The evidence wasn't there. He tried to convince his therapist he was a failure, but there just wasn't any proof.

The next session, the therapist asked Chet to write himself a letter that he imagined God would write to him.

Chet went home and started to write.

He was surprised when it became a long letter of victories, successes, moments of strong effort, even resilience. That love letter filled pages.

These two exercises challenged his dichotomous thinking.

This is also the love letter to you:

Dear Child,

You are not worthless.

You are priceless.

Love,

God

When do you use dichotomous thinking? You are either this or you are that? All or nothing?

Do you do this in your relationships? When do you use dichotomous thinking with your partner? How does this come up with your family? In your home? At your work? With yourself?

In cognitive therapy, the therapist encourages you to recognize your particular areas of faulty thinking by identifying real examples in your own life.

Now that you recognize areas of faulty thinking, what can you do about it?

Recognizing your distorted ways of thinking is a huge step! Even one insight into how you have dysfunctional thoughts is significant. If you catch yourself saying, "You always do this!" you can replace it with more accurate language of "I get so upset when you do this!"

"I am so lazy!" can be replaced with "I don't enjoy this work."

See the greater truth here?

Dysfunctional Beliefs

When you recognize your ways of thinking, you can examine the underlying beliefs that lead you down that path. Sometimes your beliefs are skewed or incorrect.

Naomi was a successful realtor. She loved her job. She loved everything about it: meeting new people, seeing beautiful homes, helping people navigate the challenges of buying, selling, moving. She loved the schedule, the professionalism. It was incredibly gratifying.

Then she met Jackson. They fell in love. They got married. He had an important job too. They bought their dream home. It was idyllic!

Then they reached the next obvious step: she got pregnant. As she neared the due date, she quit her job because good mothers stay home with their babies.

The day-to-day grind with a newborn was not great. Naomi missed her work. But she was committed to being a good mother, so she stayed home.

Days turned into months. Months into years. Another child came along. Then a third.

She didn't put the kids in preschool because good mothers stay home with their children.

When it was time for the first one to start kindergarten, Naomi had a choice. She could choose a public school, private school, or charter school. Any of those routes would have provided her the freedom to go back to work.

Naomi decided to homeschool. Why?

Because good mothers stay home with their children.

When the kids were grown and the last one had gone off to college, Naomi found herself lost and depressed.

She admitted she had been embittered, from the moment she quit her job. She resented the children for taking her away from her work. She lost her identity because she was stuck at home with kids for 22 years.

She blamed them for all of her despair, and they knew it. They hadn't asked for any of her choices, and yet they felt blamed. As a result, they felt perpetually alienated from their mother.

And why? Because she believed that good mothers stay home with their children.

Now you may be asking yourself, "Where is the problem with this belief? Isn't this true? Good mothers DO stay home with their children."

As a mother, myself, I sat in the session with her and listened to her insistence that good mothers stay home.

I said, "I am here with you right now. I am not at home with my kids. They are both in school as we speak. Based on your belief, am I not a good mother?"

"Oh no! I would never suggest that!" she exclaimed.

"So, if I am here, and you can assume I am a good mother, then what might be a more accurate belief?"

She thought for a while. After a bit she said, "*Some* good mothers stay home with their children?"

Yes. Now *that* is true.

That was where we began again. Recognizing the belief, dismantling it, restating it.

This gave her the ability to take ownership for the problem. The final step was to correct the belief and then behave differently from this moment forward.

What do good mothers do? Good mothers own their own stuff, apologize for their mistakes, make amends when possible, and try to think and behave differently from now on.

What is something you believe to be an absolute truth, but it has the potential to cause you (or others) harm? Usually, it's been engrained in your mind for years, even from childhood.

Here are a few examples, but you might have a different belief not listed here. Some beliefs are judgmental; they happen when you compare yourself to other people: "She is flawless, and I am not. There is something wrong with me."

Another belief might be an "If this…, then that…" statement. "If I do this, then a bad thing will happen." "If I leave this person, they will die." "If I take care of myself, my family will suffer."

Along these lines, you might use societal expectations to harm you: "Everyone has a college degree. What's wrong with me?" "Everyone is partnered up. I must be unlovable."

But how about these beliefs: Before I do _____, I must accomplish _____. "Before I start dating, I need to get in shape." "Before I start looking for a job I might like, I have to go back to school."

The harshest is the irreparable: "With this body/this face/these wrinkles/this brain/my illness, I will never succeed" or "…no one will want me."

Wow, you are so mean to you, my new friend!

These beliefs are usually repetitive, irrational, and they sound so familiar, as if they came from a real person (like a critical parent, a bad boss, a mean teacher, an older sibling). A client recently said, "It's like I have this tiny slave driver in my head. It's shaped a lot like my mother."

When you are confronting the dysfunctional belief, dissect it. There is a kernel of truth embedded in there, but it is wrapped in a subtle lie.

What might be your dysfunctional belief?

"I must not fail; failure is awful." Yes, it is awful. It's painful. It is embarrassing and hard. Nobody enjoys it. But does failure need to negatively define you? Have you ever learned from a failure? Did you try something and fail, only to figure out an even better solution? Have you forgiven others for their failures?

Can you change the statement slightly? Change "I must not fail; failure is awful" to "I don't like to fail because failure is hard."

Changing the belief gives you power over it. This is foundationally good for your mental health. You are telling yourself the truth. You are thinking more clearly.

In other words, if you can see the full truth of who you are, you can change your emotions, and therefore change your behaviors. How you *think* influences how you *feel,* and this influences how you *act.*

When we lie to ourselves, we feel unstable, and we react to that. When we look for the truth, we are more stable, and we respond to that. We are centered in a place of greater mental health.

Donald Meichenbaum

Donald Meichenbaum suggested we work backwards. He invites us to begin with self-observation. First, look at the problem behavior. What are you doing that is upsetting or problematic? Then, what are the emotions that drive your behavior?

Are you being short with the people around you? Acting impatient? Notice your behavior, and then stop and ask, "What am I feeling right now?"

Are you feeling disrespected, disgusted, insecure? Are you experiencing fear, sadness, abandonment, pain? Are you hungry, angry, lonely, tired?

If you sit with the emotion that fuels the behavior, explore what you are telling yourself in that emotion.

If you are angry, what are you saying in your head? "You always do this!"

If you are sad, maybe you tell yourself, "This is my life, and it will never get better."

If you are abandoned and alone, perhaps you are thinking, "Everyone leaves me. I am unlovable."

Your behaviors and your intense emotions are simply consequences, not personality flaws. They are the result of those thoughts and beliefs: of something much deeper.

Through self-reflection, conversation, and then with pen and paper, you drill down to the thoughts and beliefs you hold. Once recognized, you look for evidence. What supports and what disputes that thought?

You ask, "Who says I am are unlovable?" "What is the contrary evidence?" "Where is it written in stone?" "What is an alternative explanation for people leaving?" "Might it be them, not me?" "Might they be broken and unable to love me fully?"

When you argue against the distorted thought, you replace it. You consciously change it, and then you rehearse it. Practice the new thought, again and again, until it becomes more ingrained than the original.

We saw this in practice with Chet. He was convinced he was a failure when his depression led him to quit his job. He was challenged to look for other evidence of failures. When he couldn't, his therapist invited him to look for contrary evidence by writing the love letter from God.

Arguing against the distorted thought, Chet practiced the new information using new language. "I'm a failure" was a lie. He replaced it with "I am doing better." This is the truth.

The result? Chet had confidence to apply for and accept a new job. He has become a strong, vocal advocate for men's mental health. But to do this, he first had to change his internal dialogue.

Changing your internal dialogue can change your life.

As a reminder, this book is not intended as therapy. However, some of the ideas can feel extremely therapeutic to you.

If this chapter has triggered some deeper issues for you, you may benefit from more intensive treatment. The full therapy is called Cognitive Behavior Therapy or CBT.

CBT is shown to be one of the more widely practiced therapies. It is well researched and clinically effective. There is a QR code in the back of the book for PsychologyToday.com. Use the search tool to locate a therapist in your area. You can filter by "type of therapy." Look for CBT there.

But for the purposes of this book, let's layer the content of this chapter into your overall reflections.

Application

Breathe deep and center your focus on this topic. Reflect on how you answered past chapter questions. Now it's time to synthesize them.

- What gives your life purpose?
- What do you need?

- How are you telling your story?
- And what are you saying to yourself?
- Is there a theme emerging here?

The next set of questions may take time to fully answer.

What are some of your extreme reactions? Do you have emotional outbursts? Do you get stuck?

When these events happen, what are the thoughts that trigger these reactions?

Arbitrary inferences are conclusions we draw without evidence. When have you experienced arbitrary inferences?

Selective abstraction: When have you made yourself feel bad based on one isolated event, even in the face of a lot of contrary evidence?

Overgeneralization: Do you make huge assumptions about yourself (or others) based on a single piece of information that is not actually relevant? Can you think of examples?

Magnification: What do you magnify? Your deficits? Your flaws? Do you fixate on mistakes?

Minimization: What do you minimize? Compliments? Your skills? Your strengths? Your resilience? Your post-traumatic growth?

Personalization: What do you personalize? What are you taking on as your responsibility? What are you owning that you do not own?

Labeling: What single words do you use to define you?

Dichotomous thinking: When is your thinking black and white? Either/Or? All or nothing? Do you use words like "always," "never," "everything," "nothing?"

Now, go back over your answers to these questions.

- What is more accurate than these statements?
- How can you argue against them by telling yourself the truth?

Capture your thoughts and submit them to the truth. Telling yourself the truth helps you gain stronger mental health.

6
PERFECTIONISM
What if I fail?

What are your socials?

Me? I am a middle-aged white lady, so I'm on Facebook.

My daughter got on Instagram as a teen, so I got on just to stalk her. Now I've grown addicted. We are both on Pinterest. She tried to get me on Snapchat, but I lost interest.

I was on the platform formerly known as Twitter. It was so cool when Jimmy Fallon read one of my tweets on #hashtags.

Now I'm on TikTok. I have over 40,000 followers at the time of this writing. By the time this is published, I could have more, I could have less. TikTok might be gone. No social media platform is eternal.

I can get so lost in my socials! I will open TikTok and get absorbed for hours. I will scroll Insta and watch reels from people I've never met. I have found myself on Facebook looking at pictures of a baby of a niece of a "friend" I've never met from Orlando.

Why? I have no idea.

Social Media

Social media is powerful because you intrinsically seek connection with other human beings. Social media feels like connection. When I'm on Pinterest, I see other people share my interests, my passions. We have shared aesthetics. I feel like I belong. But most of the time, when I am on social media, I feel like I *don't* belong. I feel alienated. I feel like I'm missing out somehow.

I am slightly addicted to TikTok. It is a great source of laughter for me. Some of the people I follow are very funny. Some of them are incredibly smart. A few genuinely seek to have a voice. A couple people share their skills, their passion, their knowledge.

Many more are selling something.

Mostly they are selling insecurity. You feed on their messages, salted with "you are less than me" and peppered with "you don't measure up." So many messages telling you that you are just not enough.

The influencers make it all look so easy. Their life looks flawless. They pose themselves as transparent, authentic. So real.

In front of the camera, you see a beautiful young woman oozing confidence and contentment. Behind her mask of makeup is an internal war of insecurity and imposter syndrome.

In front of the camera, you see spotless countertops. Behind the camera, there are loads of dirty dishes, piles of clothes, open makeup tins, and spilled powders. They don't show you the stacks of unopened mail and unpaid bills. They don't display the overflowing litter boxes or the massive amounts of hair in their hairbrush. You don't see their mess.

You watch that happily married couple laughing, dancing, and teasing. Behind the smiles, there is resentment, anger, and unresolved conflict. You can't see her bitterness. You can't read his thoughts about leaving.

That couple's conflict may even be rooted in the task of needing to come up with new content every day. They argue about what is good. What is funny. How to deliver it.

They both feel pressured to keep going. They are shackled to this platform. And they will blame each other when this money stream dries up.

You watch these people who eat, sleep, and poop just like you, and you let them convince you that they are perfect and you are not.

Perfectionism

They are not perfect. Perfectionism has never been an attainable human goal. In fact, it might be a disorder.

The diagnostic and statistical manual (DSM) of the American Psychiatric Association has defined perfectionism as a form of Obsessive-Compulsive Personality Disorder. It is characterized by

> "rigid insistence on everything being flawless, perfect, without errors or faults, including one's own and others' performance; sacrificing of timeliness to ensure correctness in every detail; believing that there is only one right way to do things; difficulty changing ideas and/or viewpoint; and preoccupation with details, organization, and order."

We don't want that. We don't like rigid perfection. I don't enjoy being around people who project themselves as perfect. In fact, perfectionism in others repels us.

In her book *The Gifts of Imperfection*, Brené Brown writes,

> "Perfectionism is not the same thing has striving to be your best. Perfectionism is the belief that if we live perfect, look perfect, and act perfect, we can minimize or avoid the pain of blame, judgement, and shame. It's a shield. It's a twenty-ton shield that we lug around thinking it will protect us when, in fact, it's the thing that's really preventing us from flight."

Oh Brené. That was so good!

My maternal grandmother was "house proud." Looking back, she may have had obsessive-compulsive disorder or obsessive-compulsive personality disorder. I don't know. I was told in grad school not to diagnose family members.

You know from your own family of origin that a parent can make a demand so firmly and persuasively, you believe it's right. They insist this is a correct, moral action, and you adopt it. Even when it is irrational.

When my mother was young, my grandmother would set a cleaning kit outside each child's door on Saturday morning. The kit held a clean folded top sheet, a clean pillowcase, a feather duster, cleaning cloths, furniture polish, and window cleaner.

Before breakfast, each kid had to strip the bed, use the old top sheet as the new bottom sheet, change the pillowcase, and remake the bed with the clean sheet on top. Then they washed their windows, dusted every surface in the room, including the baseboards behind the bed and dresser, and polished all the wood. They did this every Saturday before breakfast.

After breakfast, and for the rest of the day, the girls scrubbed every other room of the house. The boys mowed and trimmed the lawn and weeded the gardens. They washed the cars and swept the garage floor. They even washed the driveway.

To perfection.

Guess what my mother learned from her childhood routines? Houses had to be spotless in order to be livable.

Guess what I learned.

Same.

And I never questioned it!

When my kids were little, I would wake up on Saturdays and frenetically clean. I treated my kids like an imposition. They were an obstacle to my goals.

I remember my sister called me one Saturday morning. I answered the phone only to bitterly complain to her that I had just swept the kitchen floor and the baby and the kitten were both rolling around in the dirt pile.

She laughed and said, "Enjoy these moments, Melissa."

I hung up on her.

I was so insistent that my frantic cleaning was normal that my husband stopped trying to argue with me. Instead, he gathered up the kids, got them dressed, and took them out to breakfast on Saturdays.

They would go to the park after that. They'd visit the zoo, the farmers market, the mall, the children's museum. They'd feed ducks in our pond or ride horses on the gateway trail behind our barn. They indulged in a lazy Saturday. They had fun!

I had asphyxiation from the bathroom bleach.

After Scott passed away, I did some hard soul-searching about how I had spent my time and energy when he was alive.

I could have listened to him. I could have thought critically about the messages passed down from my grandmother. I could have seen the perfectionism as insanity instead of legacy.

We could have lived in squalor. My kids would not have remembered the mess. But they do remember the crazy cleaning of a frenetic mother.

Striving for perfection is bad for your mental health. It is toxic. It's hard on your relationships. And it is impossible to attain.

No, those influencers you religiously watch on your socials are not perfect. That young woman with the 27-step process of putting on her morning makeup is actually quite pretty before she starts with the primer. And yet, watching her striving for the appearance of perfection, we start to feel like we aren't enough.

I would not be surprised if you struggle with an internal demand that you be _____ enough. Good enough. Smart enough. Pretty enough. Sexy enough. Wealthy enough. You can fill in the blank for yourself.

What will be enough? When will *you* be enough? How will your life be different when you decide you have enough? When you decide you are enough? How will life be different when you are simply content?

You are barraged with messages from everywhere telling us that we aren't enough. If you google "how many ads does a person see in a day 2023" the number is 10,000 advertisements.

That may be a bit excessive, but I am certain we see at least 100 or more active advertising campaigns a day. They are on billboards and sides of buses. They pop up before we can stream something. We are hit with sponsored posts on your social media platforms, each campaign telling us that we are not enough. We must be better.

Rational Emotive Behavior Therapy (REBT)

Albert Ellis created a therapy called Rational Emotive Behavior Therapy (REBT). Like Beck and Meichenbaum, Ellis thought people contribute to their own psychological problems.

Ellis said we hold rigid, extreme beliefs about ourselves, others, and about life. Epictetus agrees: "People are disturbed not by events, but by the views which they take of them."

Musts

Ellis posited three basic musts that you might believe and any one of these demands can cause you distress:

1. *I must do well.* I must be perfect, successful, well-liked, fill in the blank.
2. *You must treat me well.* You must be fair, kind, loving toward me; you must recognize my value, you must respect me, etc.
3. *Life must be good.* Life must be easy, hassle free. Life must be comfortable, gratifying, happy, painless, and so on.

These all sound reasonable, right? But they are dangerous.

Why? Well, let's unpack them one by one.

I must do well.

What does "do well" mean? Are we talking academically? Professionally? And by whose standards must I do well?

What does "successful" mean? A mansion, a boat, a closet full of designer shoes? Or is success measured in kindness and love and intimate relationship?

And "well-liked" by whom? Do you have specific names?

You must treat me well.

Why? Why must you be treated well? And how do you control for this? How do you make this happen? How do you make everyone treat you well?

And that last one? *Life must be good.*

Well, that is a doozy of a demand.

A client flounced into my office one day, dramatically collapsed on the couch, and in complete exasperation, complained, "Why can't life just be easy?!"

Of course, a good therapist always answers a question with another question.

I asked, "Who do you know whose life is easy?"

She paused, looked at me, thought hard. Finally, she slumped down and muttered, "Oprah."

Good one.

Seriously, who has a life that is free of stress? Who doesn't have pain? Who isn't worried about something? Whose life is free from sadness, angst, or loss?

Why should you be any different from the rest of us?

Ellis would say the problem begins with the demanding language and the ambiguity around expectations.

But if you are demanding you be this, and you lack specificity around the expectations, you will always fall short. You must be successful, but you don't really know what you mean by that, so how do you even get there?

Besides, who says you must be perfect/successful/well-liked/fill-in-the-blank? Where is it written in stone that others treat you well?

Why do you believe life must be easy for you? It has never been easy for a single other human being in the history of our species.

Okay, so you see there's a problem here. But it gets even more problematic and painful when you complete the rest of each sentence:

1. *I must do well (I* must be perfect, successful, well-liked, fill in the blank) *or I am a failure, a loser, a joke, an imposter.*
2. *You must treat me well* (you must be fair, kind, loving, respectful, and recognize me) *or you are a failure, a loser, a joke, an imposter unworthy of me.*
3. *Life must be good* (life must be easy, painless, comfortable, and happy) *or I will be miserable and overwhelmed. If life isn't good, it isn't worth living.*

Well, that escalated quickly.

You create this dialectic: "I'm either perfect, or I'm a failure. I'm either good, or I'm evil. Life is either excellent, or life is worthless." Does this remind you of CBT? They are definitely related.

Like CBT, Ellis invites you to become aware of your irrational beliefs. Then test them with questions of "where does this come from? Or "who says??

Next, you recognize the problematic word in each demand. See if you can spot the word that's causing all the ruckus?

1. *I must do well.*
2. *You must treat me well.*
3. *Life must be good.*

Do you see it?

Must.

MUST!

My colleague Kenny calls it "musterbation."

Don't blame me. I'm just the messenger.

He's the one who said it.

Preferences

Next, we replace it with a different word. Watch:

1. *I ~~must~~ do well.*
   I prefer to do well.
2. *You ~~must~~ treat me well.*
   I prefer that you treat me well.
3. *Life ~~must~~ be good.*
   I prefer that life is good.

Well, now! Look at that!

Where you were choking yourself with a vice-like grip of demands and musts, now you can breathe a bit easier by stating your preferences.

Stating your preferences allows you to hold things much more loosely in your hands. You can exhale and say, "I hope I do well" and "I prepared for this" or "My success rests in my effort, not the outcome." Progress over perfection, my friend!

Imagine how you could change your relationships if you thought, "I prefer you treat me well, but I can love you even when you don't."

What if you acknowledged that, while you prefer life be stress free, it isn't right now? You could think more clearly about the situation. You could admit that you have the skills and resources (and this book) to help you manage it.

There are other words that can hold you captive. I encourage you to listen for them: *can't, too hard, impossible, have to, only.* Words are powerful weapons and can do a lot of damage. Changing them can set you free.

Changing your beliefs, your demands, your language can change you. It can change your relationships. It can change your life. And it can change your mental health.

Just remember, it takes practice.

Karen Horney and the Tyranny of the Should

Speaking of changing your language, German psychoanalyst Karen Horney had a phrase called "the tyranny of the should."

You know how this works: you tell yourself, "I should exercise more." "I should leave five minutes earlier every morning so I'm not running late for work." "I should finish that painting." "I should send a card to my aunt and uncle." "I should trim those hedges." "I should be nicer to my brother-in-law."

I should. I know. Sorry, John.

Just like Ellis' "musts," the word "should" implies that you have an obligation to complete an action. There will be a consequence if you fail to do so.

"Should" is making a demand on you, but not carrying any actions along with it. "Should" holds some sort of moral imperative, but no plan.

You might think, "I should spend more time with my grandparents." But that wasn't an actual decision. You didn't follow up with an action or schedule or strategy. So it didn't happen.

But you mentally abuse yourself because you didn't spend time with your grandparents.

"Should" is a very bad boss.

I know what you're thinking: "Okay... so what should I do about that?"

Ha! Caught that!

But also, great question!

Just like replacing "musts" with preferences, replace the word "should" with "could." "Should" could become "want to" or "will try to" or even "choose to...."

I could exercise more.

I want to finish that painting.

I will try to get up earlier tomorrow so I can get to work on time.

I choose to be more tolerant of my brother-in-law when he is annoying.

"Could," "want to," "will try," and "choose" inherently carry a decision or action with them.

You'll notice, with practice, the word "should" will disappear and you find yourself developing different habits.

You get the picture. Should is not a good word.

As my colleague Kenny says, "Stop 'shoulding' on yourself."

He's gross, right?

Wabi-Sabi

When my husband was diagnosed with lung cancer, I had just started taking a pottery class at my university. He was sick for 4 ½ months, and during that time, I made some of the ugliest pottery you will ever see. Circles are hard. Clay doesn't always do what you want it to. It is noncooperative. There are rules clay forces you to follow.

But I found it to be so therapeutic. My tears of dread and despair would drop into the clay, and the clay simply absorbed them. My tears became part of the vessel I was making.

My sadness became heaviness in the bottoms of the mugs. My fears showed up in the edges. My future felt as fragile as my mug handles. My pottery displayed the truth of my heart.

I complained to Heather, my ceramics teacher, that my pottery was so ugly. She said, "No, Melissa, it isn't ugly. Your pottery is *wabi-sabi*."

I don't know where I found the actual definition, but now I use *wabi-sabi* to describe the beauty of imperfection.

You see it everywhere. The asymmetrical freckles on the most beautiful face you look at every day. The imperfect balance of the tree out in front of your home. The impermanence of a ripe orange. The resilience of that dandelion that grows out of a crack in the sidewalk.

It has been years since he died, and my pottery is still *wabi-sabi*. There is not a perfect mug or bowl or vase yet to come out of my kiln. But if you want a perfect mug, you can buy one at the dollar store, pressed from a mold and exactly like the other 20 mugs behind it on the shelf. If you want something that is beautifully imperfect, look at ceramic pieces made by a potter.

By the way, the process for making a pottery piece is a great analogy for life. You can skip ahead to the chapter application if you want, but you might also find this a lovely metaphor.

First, the clay is literally dug up from the ground. It is the most natural substance brought up out of the earth.

When I begin, I slice a chunk of clay off of the larger slab. Usually, I use a wire to cut through it; sometimes I will use a knife for smaller pieces. Sometimes I just pinch off a big hunk of it. It's a fairly abrupt and violent severing from the parent slab.

Then I wedge the smaller lump of clay. Wedging clay is much like kneading bread. I use the palms of my hands to push it while my fingers pull it towards me. Wedging forces all the air bubbles and impurities to the surface, so they can be released and not mar the final piece. The pressure refines it.

Then I mold the clay, rolling in on the board and slapping it into a ball with my palms.

Next, I literally throw that ball onto my pottery wheel, hoping to get it as close to center as possible. The pressure of throwing it on the wheel creates a suction, adhering the ball to the wheel.

As the wheel begins to turn, I pour water over the clay to reduce friction between my hands and the clay. With my fingers and palms, I create firm but gentle pressure on the lump of clay, centering it on the wheel. During this process I concentrate on my breathing and savor the roughness of the grit in the clay.

With my eyes closed, I feel the part of the clay that is out of balance and apply extra pressure to that area as it spins under my hands.

When the clay is fully centered, I study it. It will appear as though it is not moving, even though it is whirling around at high speed. It will look like a smooth-sided, flat-topped thick disc of clay.

Next, I dribble a little more water on the top, firmly place my hands around the thick disk, and gently press my thumb down into the center. As I do this, the center gives way and opens up. I press down further and pull my thumb slightly outwards, creating the interior of the cup or bowl or whatever I am making.

As I mold this, I never lose contact between my two hands. They are constantly touching. If I touch the spinning clay with only one hand, I risk throwing the entire thing off balance.

As the wheel turns quickly, I press my fingers against the interior wall of the cup while also pressing against the outside. Lifting my hands together creates height and thins out the walls. I do this a few times.

Using firm and consistent pressure against the clay, my hands have formed the shape and size.

As it continues to spin, I smooth it out. I'll close my eyes and feel the walls, from bottom to top, to determine and adjust thickness. I might squeeze an area to create a curve. I might press the interior to bow it out and create roundness.

I will apply gentle pressure to the top to smooth the lip. I can apply my fingernail to the sides to form spirals on the outside. I will press the tip of my pinky finger to the bottom to create a foot.

When the clay has shown me what it is able and willing to become, I slide a wire under the piece to release it from the wheel. I gently lift it and place it on a drying board. Then I wait.

Hours later, when it is leather hard (the texture and firmness of a leather belt), I will gently place it upside down, center it on a clean bat (a plate that attaches to my pottery wheel), affix it to the bat with some clean, soft lumps of clay to hold it down, and begin to trim it.

Trimming means using a sharp tool to cut away the excess clay that makes the cup too heavy or too misshapen. Trimming smooths the clay and gives it the final shape. To finish this stage, I will carve my initials into the bottom or stamp it with my little honeybee logo.

Then I flip it up, place it on a clean, dry surface and attach a handle. The handle is usually a lump of clay I have held in my hand and pulled into a handle shape using firm hand pressure and a water bath. Sometimes the handle is carved out of the parent slab. Sometimes I get creative and make something completely ridiculous, like braided clay ropes or a rolled slice of clay.

Using a sharp tool, I will scratch the surface of the mug where I want the ends of the handle to go. Then I scratch up the edges of the handle where it will stick to the mug. I use a slip, a thin film made from clay and water to slather on the scratched-up areas.

I attach the handle, slip to slip, and hold it all together for a few seconds until the handle is affixed.

I admire it. Adjust it slightly. Nod approvingly.

I cover the mug for a day to even out the moisture level of the cup and handle, then I let it dry completely.

When it is dry, it looks great. It looks like you could drink from it. It feels hard to the touch; it has a sturdy heft in your hand. But if I flick it with my fingernail, it sounds like a small "thud" instead of a lovely "ping."

If I pinch the lip of it lightly, I will easily snap off a piece. The handle will easily break off. I can squeeze the mug in my hand, and the whole thing will shatter.

Dried clay is not strong clay.

To make it strong, I must fire it. Bisque firing means placing my beautiful little mug in a kiln and heating it to 1828 degrees Fahrenheit. That is 998 degrees Celsius. It gets red hot. It takes about 24 hours from start of the firing to being cool to the touch again.

When it has been fired to this temperature, it is now sturdy and strong. I can't break it unless I throw it against a cement wall. It is oven ready, microwave safe. It's great.

Except it is not functional. It still can't hold liquid. It is porous, water permeable. I can't use it for much of anything except maybe holding loose change. A bisque-fired mug is useless until I dress it.

So, I glaze the mug. Glaze is a glassy coating, applied as a liquid, dried to a powder, and then fired. Glaze makes the mug impermeable to water and makes the mug even harder.

It also makes the mug beautiful!

So, I have to paint on some glaze. I usually combine colors, layering one over another or paint one above the other so they can melt into one another. I never know what the final piece will look like.

When I first paint them on, blue glazes might dry pink. Green glazes can look red. Brown glazes might dry grey. Clear glazes dry white. All of the glazes dry into a chalky film. Looking at them before they go into the kiln, I never know what I'm going to get when it's all done.

I put these ugly, gloopy, chalky pieces back in the kiln, and fire it even hotter. The colors meld together best at 2190 degrees Fahrenheit (1198 C), but I can fire as high as 2300 degrees Fahrenheit (1260 C).

Again, I watch the temps ramp up to red heat, I wait for it to hold, and then watch the temperature slowly drop as the pieces cool. It feels achingly long to wait.

My kiln is in my garage, and I open the garage doors in the morning when I know everything will be cool to the touch. I want to get the best light to see my new creations.

I gently lift the kiln lid, prop it open, and am amazed at the glittering mugs winking at me in the sunlight.

As I lift each one out, I study it. I see every single imperfection. The glazes are too thick here. They didn't even adhere to the clay there. That glaze formed tiny bubbles or pock marks. This is a weird color. Here is a chip I forgot to smooth out on the handle. The top isn't perfectly round. The bottom is too thick and heavy.

Each one is imperfect. Each one is beautiful. Each one is *wabi-sabi*.

So are you. You have endured pressure and heat. You have been refined. You are imperfect and beautiful. You are *Wabi-sabi*.

Application

Let's take a break here to reflect. With as much honesty and insight as you can muster, begin to journal.

- What are your areas of perfectionistic demands?
- Where do they come from?
- How does your perfectionism help you or harm you?
- What are your "musts"? Writing them out, use the word "must" as the anchor.
- How can you replace each sentences using "prefer" or "want" or "would like to"?
- When are you using the word "should"? What word(s) are you most likely to use to replace "should"?
- And can you embrace your imperfection?
- Might you get *wabi-sabi* tattooed on your wrist?

7
POST-TRAUMATIC GROWTH
Where is my resilience?

My kids and I have been in therapy. A lot.

We each have an individual therapist, and we share a family therapist, Roger.

Good ole Rog.

I searched for Roger for a long time. I knew we needed someone skilled in Dialectical Behavior Therapy (DBT), who understood trauma, and who could work with our broken little family.

We have been through some hard stuff. We needed someone who could teach us how to work together through our shared trauma.

I am certain you've endured trauma, too. You probably thought this was just your life. Maybe you assumed it's not a big deal. Everyone endures hard stuff.

That may very well be true.

However, your trauma is still significant. And it might be stalling you from moving forward.

Trauma Theory

Sometimes we hear about "Big T" Trauma and "little t" trauma. A quick description: Big T Trauma is related to life-threatening events or events that threaten serious harm.

We experience this kind of trauma when we are the victims of violence, endure a natural disaster, survive a mass shooting, or are devasted by the sudden, unexpected death of a loved one, especially one's child. It is especially traumatizing when the death is violent or self-imposed. It is also Big T when we witness the trauma of another person close to us.

"Little t" trauma usually doesn't involve violence or disaster but can still be extremely upsetting. You might experience this form of trauma through a breakup or being forced out of a friend group. Your parents' divorce, the death of a pet, a major job loss, or an academic failure can be traumatic.

It might surprise you that chronic exposure to smaller traumatic events can cause more psychological harm than exposure to one big traumatic event.

The Diathesis Stress Model

It may also surprise you that many major mental illnesses emerge following a traumatic event.

Most of us are born with genetic predispositions to certain illnesses, both mental and physical. Our biological families pass down genomic tendencies for certain cancers or genetic anomalies. They can also pass on heritability for mood disorders, anxiety disorders, schizophrenic spectrum disorders, and so on.

The diathesis stress model of mental illness holds that these disorders can lie dormant until a stressor or traumatic event kicks the disease into gear. You may have no family history of schizophrenia, but your epigenetics can predispose you to it.

Then the death of a parent or a hard breakup can trigger a first episode psychosis. Depression, anxiety, panic—whatever you are predisposed to, the stressor may allow it to emerge. The trauma doesn't have to be "big T" trauma, but often a major stressor of some kind precedes the first experience of a major mental illness.

Trauma that triggers the start of a mental illness can be physical as well as emotional or psychological. An intense marijuana high has been found to trigger a first episode of psychosis. A urinary tract infection can cause hallucinations and delusions among the elderly. Depression and suicidality have been linked to repeated concussions in athletes.

And this may surprise you, but strep can be traumatic for children.

A child with a streptococcal infection like strep throat or scarlet fever may develop a sudden and severe mental illness. Usually this emerges as an obsessive-compulsive disorder (OCD). Tic disorders are also common. Sometimes a child develops both.

A parent may notice the child's behaviors suddenly change with strep. It is often a sudden and surprising turn.

This mental illness may manifest in checking behaviors, new hand-washing rituals, rigid routines, repetitive behaviors, and increased fearfulness. The child may develop vocal or physical tics. They may even show new separation anxiety when away from close family members or away from home.

Unfortunately, these behaviors do not go away with the antibiotics that treat the strep. Your child will require active treatment with some combination of psychotropic medication and Exposure and Response Prevention (ERP) strategies designed to address OCD.

If you are curious to learn more about this, you can research PANDAS, which stands for Pediatric Autoimmune Neuropsychiatric Disorders Associated with Streptococcal Infections.

Mental illnesses can be triggered by trauma. While sometimes it is a physical trauma, it is more likely emotional or psychological trauma stemming from an event or an ongoing situation.

There are three main types of traumas: Acute, Chronic, or Complex.

Acute Trauma

My husband was working as a director out in Los Angeles. One night one of his rehearsals ran late. It was dark, he hadn't eaten much all day, and he was craving a couple chili dogs. He pulled into a gas station in a pretty rough area near the rehearsal site before getting onto the 405 to head home.

As he pulled away from the station, he was carjacked. He admitted later that he was stupid to put up a fight. His resistance resulted in a brutal beating from the guys taking his car.

He survived, but with severe physical trauma: torn retina, multiple bones broken in his face. He needed reconstructive surgery with titanium plates and pins to put him back together again.

He was my Humpty Dumpty.

This was an acute trauma. He really thought he was going to die.

Acute trauma is an isolated traumatic event. It is severe, violent, life-threatening. According to the National Institute of Mental Health, acute trauma is often connected with short-term post-traumatic stress disorder.

Acute trauma is hard to process, and many will have what we call an "acute stress reaction." This usually lasts less than 48 hours.

We are shaken up, we talk about it, we cry, we ruminate, we sweat a lot. We feel panicked. We may even feel detached from ourselves, as if we are watching things as an outsider. These are all normal responses to acute trauma.

Chronic Trauma

Chronic trauma is repeated, prolonged events. Bullying, childhood abuse or neglect, and domestic violence are traumatic and ongoing. Watching another person, especially a loved one, endure constant abuse can also be a form of chronic trauma.

Starvation, deprivation, war, and ongoing human atrocities are horrific and chronic. Even a chronic illness requiring invasive medical procedures can be chronic trauma.

When I was alone in Los Angeles, I ran out of money. I was too sick from an undiagnosed and untreated autoimmune disease to work. I lived in the back seat of my car.

I parked my car in an empty lot between a bakery and a church. I lived on stale bread out of the bakery dumpster. I had a jar of peanut butter and a bucket of honey. The church gave me access to the restroom and shower in their gymnasium.

Every day I'd find a place of shade to stay out of sight and stay cool. Every night I'd hide in the back seat of my car.

Because of the area I found myself in, sirens became my white noise. Helicopters hovered over me. Their spotlights scanned the streets around me.

Gunshots punctured the night.

I experienced serious, significant traumatic events. My children have asked that I someday write a book about my life, but I am reluctant. The thought of writing out some of these stories makes my hands literally tremble. There is a lot I have yet to unpack with my own trauma therapist.

But here's the thing. The trauma was chronic and painful. But I was not a child when these things happened to me. And the traumatic events were not personal. They were not in the context of a family, community, or "protective" relationship.

Complex Trauma

When a child is exposed to chronic abuse or neglect, this is complex trauma. This kind of trauma is often violent, invasive, and/or interpersonal in nature.

Community violence, racism, discrimination, and war cause complex trauma in children as well.

The key features of complex trauma are threefold:

1) the trauma happens in the child's relationships;

2) the trauma impacts the child's development (emotionally, psychologically, socially, or physically); and

3) the trauma is chronic or repeated. The child feels like they cannot escape it.

Was this you? Did people who were entrusted to protect you fail to do that?

If so, this might be the work you can do to enhance your mental health. Please continue reading this chapter all the way to the end.

Stress Disorders

When you experience a trauma, especially an acute trauma, you may develop Acute Stress Disorder (ASD) within the first month of a trauma. When symptoms last for more than a month, the diagnosis changes to post-traumatic stress disorder (PTSD).

Surprisingly, the symptoms of PTSD might not emerge until long after the trauma occurred. A domestic violence survivor might develop symptoms years after the violence has ended. Some Vietnam vets developed PTSD after they retired from their careers.

The symptoms are the same for both acute stress and post-traumatic disorders. You re-experience the trauma. You might have flashbacks, nightmares, physical signs of stress, or distressing thoughts or emotions.

You will avoid places or events that remind you of the experience. You will avoid thoughts that lead to intense feelings about the event. You will experience hyper-arousal: you might be easily startled.

You might feel chronically tense and unable to relax. You have difficulty sleeping or concentrating. You feel angry or aggressive.

With PTSD, you might have exaggerated self-blame by assuming you somehow deserved the trauma.

You might withdraw from others or have negative thoughts about the world. You might even have difficulty feeling positive emotion.

We often see people with serious trauma and PTSD comparing their trauma to others, believing theirs isn't quite as severe as other peoples' trauma. Please remember this isn't a contest. Your trauma is trauma, unrelated to anyone else's.

How to find trauma-informed care

If you are experiencing symptoms of acute stress disorder or post-traumatic stress disorder, please seek assistance from a licensed mental health professional. Look for one who is skilled in trauma-informed care.

Because this is particularly important to me that you get help, I will give you direct access to resources here. Here is the recipe:

1. Visit www.psychologytoday.com on your laptop or tablet. Or
   a. Go to the back of this book.
   b. Find the QR code for Psychology Today.
   c. Scan the code with your phone.
2. To locate therapists in your area, put in your zip code.
3. In the drop-down menu of "Issues" you will search for "Trauma and PTSD." You may have to look under "see more issues" to find it.
4. Under the "type of therapy" drop-down, look for Brainspotting, EMDR, and/or trauma-focused therapies.
5. Review the therapists who come up from that search.

You might also go through your insurance provider to see who is covered. Your workplace may have an Employee Assistance Program that covers your treatment.

If all the therapists have waitlists or are booking a few months out, that's okay. Get on the list. Make the appointment for a few months from now. Make a bunch of appointments with different therapists and see which one you get in to see the soonest. Then go back and cancel the other appointments.

The longer you wait to make the appointment, the longer you wait to feel better. You deserve to feel better as soon as possible. Get yourself on the lists.

If you are in a rural area, you may need to broaden your range to a couple hundred miles. These are relatively quick therapies, usually brief and very effective, so you will not likely be making this drive for years. There may even be providers in metropolitan areas in your state that offer therapy virtually, so you won't have to drive at all.

There is encouraging research confirming these alternative therapies work. While "talk therapy" is useful for a lot of disorders, it isn't always as effective for treating trauma as others like brainspotting, eye-movement desensitization and retraining (EMDR), or accelerated resolution therapy (ART).

Also, these alternative therapies might not require you to repeatedly talk through your trauma in great detail. They can feel emotionally "safer" because you don't have to continually revisit the pain.

Resilience

If you have endured a trauma and you are reading this book, you are remarkably resilient.

Resilience is enduring and processing hard events. It is being flexible under high pressure.

Picture a palm tree in a hurricane: the tree bends under the strong winds. Sometimes it bends all the way to the ground. When the cyclone ends, the tree stands tall again.

If that's you, I applaud you! Your resilience is powerful, especially when you *feel* like you are breaking.

And I can probably guess what has contributed to your resilience. You probably have some solid problem-solving skills. Maybe you took control of the situation. Perhaps you asked for help. These are proven factors of resilience.

Maybe you had someone in your corner who saw you through. You knew you could count on them if you needed them. You were resilient because you had a good therapist, a kind teacher, a supportive family member, a strong community, or a loving church. In other words, you were resilient because you had social support.

Perhaps you were resilient because you had some level of self-compassion. You allowed yourself to react to it. You knew you didn't deserve that trauma.

It's even more likely you were resilient if you gave yourself the space and time to work through it. Your resilience came from emotional intelligence. You were able to feel your emotions without shutting them down. Perhaps you could name your feelings when you needed to. You could say, "I'm mad!" "I'm scared." "I'm hurt."

It's likely you were resilient when you could self-soothe when your emotions became intense.

Maybe you were resilient because you knew that you would endure this, no matter what you suffered. You understood you didn't really have a choice, so you muscled through and survived it.

You trusted that you had survived trauma before—and that you would survive again. You trusted yourself to overcome this too.

And finally, I suspect you were resilient because you were optimistic that someday it would get better. You held on until it was.

This list of factors, my friend, is the recipe for resilience.

Post-Traumatic Growth

Now I'm taking it a step further.

After the trauma, some people emerge into post-traumatic growth. Maybe this is you too.

You've heard powerful stories of people who are paralyzed, and—through sheer will and resolve—they learn to walk again. You've heard about people who are diagnosed with cancer but credit a strong faith and a good attitude to recover and find a new zest for life.

You know of the person who loses both legs in combat, and in spite of the catastrophic loss of limbs, they emerge like a phoenix out of the ashes.

Maybe this is you, but you rose out of the ashes of a mental challenge. Maybe you have emerged out of psychological or emotional harm.

Even with the hard experiences and the emotions that came with them, you developed a new understanding of yourself. With time, dedication, energy, and resolve, you found a sense of personal transformation.

You have learned how to relate to other people, even in their own trauma story.

There is an inventory called the Post-Traumatic Growth Inventory (PTGI) developed by Tedeschi and Calhoun.

The assessment looks at five areas of personal development after trauma: appreciation of life, enhanced relationship with others, seeing new possibilities in life, personal strength, and spiritual change.

A number of years after my husband died, I started dating again.

I know. Like I hadn't suffered enough already.

One of the initial questions I would ask each first date was, "What happened to your last relationship?"

Then I would listen as they would tell the story. She was crazy. She was never happy. She was verbally abusive. She was to blame.

Some guys were clueless. They had no idea why their marriage ended. Everything seemed fine, and then they were divorced.

Not a single man ever said to me on the first date, "It was my fault."

And then I met Hamish. He was kind, well-dressed, chivalrous. He was well-educated and successful. He was tall, handsome, and intense.

Okay, I'll just say it. He was so hot.

When I asked the question, "What happened to your last relationship?" he went quiet. He paused, reflected, and then thoughtfully nodded.

He said, "I was not there for her. She did all the heavy lifting in our marriage. I hid away in my office. I was mopey when I did not get regular sex. I was petulant when I had to help out with the kids. I didn't do chores around the house unless forced. I was easily annoyed, and I'd yell a lot."

He continued, "I would make grand gestures—give expensive gifts, big trips, great surprises—when she threatened to leave. But I never really listened to what she wanted. I didn't hear what she was asking of me. I didn't change to be the partner she needed."

Wow! That was insightful and honest!

Much later he told the rest of the story: the marriage ended when she met someone at work. She had an affair that lasted a couple of years. When he found out, he felt completely bereft and betrayed. She left him and married the other man.

The infidelity was traumatic to him. But he didn't lead off with that. In response to the question of why he was single, he didn't lay blame.

This man had done some hard self-exploration. He recognized his own contributions to the demise of the relationship. He took ownership of the problem. He committed to never be that person again.

This was someone who unpacked his own baggage and washed his dirty laundry.

From there, he worked on improving himself in other areas. He started exercising daily, returned to the church and developed a devout faith. He attended years of therapy to work on emotional intelligence and communication skills.

Now he responds to conflict instead of reacting to it. He wants to give himself to a relationship without keeping score.

Of course I married him.

Did I mention he was hot?

Post-traumatic growth is also using your pain and trauma to help others. I'll use my son as an example.

In a very short period of time, my son had endured too many losses. His dad had died. Then we had to put down Sam's dog Odie. Then Sam's horse coliced (developed a sudden and severe abdominal condition) and died. Two of Sam's cousins died. And the uncle, the one who had stepped in as a father figure, passed away.

So when Sam was in 9th grade and he asked if he could throw a weekend Halloween party, of course I said yes. He thought he'd invite about ten kids over.

About 1:00 pm, they started showing up: a shark, Captain America, a pirate, Elsa, a witch, Harry Potter, a scarecrow, Darth Vader, an accident victim on crutches, a prom queen with a cleaver in her head.

I didn't recognize any of these kids. I'd not met any of them before. Completely new crowd.

The party started. Music emanated from the basement. The talking grew louder. The laughing increased.

There was dancing. There was karaoke. There were video games and loud jokes and a lot of running through the house.

Cases of soda emptied. Cascades of chips and popcorn consumed. I had to order pizza twice.

The last one was picked up at 1 in the morning. These strangers had been in my house for 12 hours.

The next day, as we cleaned up, Sam and I chatted.

Me: "Did you have fun last night?"

Sam: "Yeah! I had a blast!"

Me: "Good! (pause) Um, who were those people? I didn't recognize any of them."

Sam: "Oh! Yeah. Well, the kid in the shark costume? He never gets picked as a partner in science. The kid with the crutches has something going on with his legs so he doesn't walk great. Harry Potter is autistic. That girl in the prom dress is always sitting alone at lunch…."

He listed how each kid was alone in their 9th grade class.

Sam had been through so much at such a young age. And because he knew pain, he could see pain in the kids around him.

While he had a strong group of friends, he noticed that these kids did not. He brought them all together at our house, and by the time they left, they had their own established friend group.

Fast forward five years and the experiment is still a success. Those kids stay in touch. They get together on breaks home from college.

Trauma is a common human experience. None of us get out of this life unscathed. What does the Dread Pirate Roberts say in *The Princess Bride*? "Life is pain, Highness. Anyone who says differently is selling something."

We can't avoid pain. But for better mental health, you can use it for growth.

Application

This is a difficult topic, and you have persevered. I applaud you. Now it's time to dig a bit deeper. Take a deep breath, pick up your pen, and ponder.

Post-traumatic growth doesn't happen in place of your pain. It happens *because of* your pain.

- What are your Big T and small t experiences with trauma?
- As you look back over them, when did you demonstrate resilience?
- What contributed to that resilience?
- What helped you bounce back instead of break?
- When have you used your painful experiences for growth?

- Where have you seen others use their pain for greater purpose?
- How can you use your pain to find your purpose?

8
POTENTIAL
What is my power?

"What is the most powerful thing you can do right now?"

"Forgive him."

Let me give you a little background on the theory, and then I'll tell you the whole story.

I need to caution you first. You may bristle at the word "feminist" because it feels threatening to you somehow. Or you may embrace feminism and think I am too soft on the definition.

Either way, I am using the term "feminist" from an academic, theoretical perspective. I am applying the therapeutic version of the theory. Please know that my use of the term "feminism" must be untethered from your personal and political views and opinions. Please keep an open mind. To quote Inigo Montoya, "I do not think it means what you think it means."

Feminist Theory

When I first taught on feminist theory, I liked it. So many of the theories I've mentioned up to the point only look at what is happening inside your head. I appreciate that this theory recognizes that we don't function in a vacuum. Feminist theory explores what is happening on the outside as well.

In fact, the ways in which you struggle are often tied to other people and the roles you are assigned.

What do I mean by "roles?"

You are a wage earner for the family. You are an employee. You are the boss. You are a partner to your significant other. You are the child to your parents. You are the parent to your children.

Wage earner, employee, boss, child, partner, parent: these are all roles you fill. Each role holds certain rules or expectations for you.

Each of these roles is influenced, at least in part, by your gender. As wage earner, are you receiving equal pay for your work? As an employee, are you receiving the same opportunities for promotion? Does your gender influence the tasks you are assigned? If you are a strong leader, do others call you a boss or a female dog?

As a partner, does your gender inform what the other person expects of you? Do you have to give more energy than they do in terms of chores, mental load, financial load, or emotional load in the partnership?

If you are a parent, how much is your gender going to affect the distribution of time and energy expended in parenting? If you divorce, will your gender determine how much time you will be allowed to spend with your children or how much child support you will be required to pay?

While we are trying to create greater equity in all of these roles, there are still cultural and familial expectations around how we fulfill our roles because of our gender. In a faith community, there may be expectations for gendered expression based on church doctrines.

In the US, there are "gender reveal" parties for expectant parents, but what they are revealing is the biological sex, not the socialized rules and roles of gender that the family will apply after the baby is born.

Many of us resist being so narrowly defined by social expectations of our biological sex. Women can be strong, independent, and complex. Men can be tender, interdependent, and multifaceted. Women can be rational; men can be emotional.

Therapists who use feminist theory recognize that traditional gender roles have restricted our freedom as men and women. In the simplest of terms, feminist theory wants all genders to have equal rights and opportunities. Feminism embraces the radical notion that, unrelated to our gender, we are all human beings.

Power

Now, back to the question "What's the most powerful thing you can do?" Feminist theory talks about power—what is it, who has it, who doesn't, where is it, and how is it expressed?

Power isn't found in hammers or fists. Power is not physical might or relational aggression. Power, according to William Glasser, in his Choice Theory, comes from making a difference. Your power comes from leaving a legacy. Power comes through influence, impact, significance.

Natalie was raised by a single mother. She never met her dad.

Natalie's mom had to work a lot to support the two of them. They didn't have much money, and Natalie spent a lot of time alone. She didn't witness a marriage; she didn't see how a healthy relationship worked. She never lived with another person except for a mom who was gone a lot. And because her mom was working so hard, Natalie didn't get a lot of active parenting either.

But Natalie did well. She had friendships in school and stayed active and engaged in her community.

Eventually, she met someone and fell in love. They got married. Nine months later, they had a son, and six years later, another one.

Natalie is a good mother. She is tender, nurturing, attentive, fun. She doesn't yell. She meets her sons' needs and she allows them space. She celebrates their victories and honors their failures. She's a very good mom.

She is also a good spouse. She works very hard. She is supportive of him. She laughs at his jokes. She tolerates his flaws. She doesn't over-correct or attempt to control him. She genuinely respects him and acts lovingly towards him.

Natalie had a choice. She could have repeated the family legacy of single parenting. She could have burned through hard relationships with difficult men. She could have sought to gain mastery over her own paternal abandonment by attempting to keep men who didn't want to stay.

But instead, Natalie took her absence of relationships and intentionally curated ones that fulfilled her. She created new relationships that are deep, loving, and long-lasting. She has made a profound impact on her children, and with firm support and respect, she has encouraged her husband to become his best self.

This is Natalie's legacy. This is the most powerful thing she could do, and she has done it incredibly well.

What is the most powerful thing you can do in the circumstances you find yourself in? What are your choices? Here is an extreme example.

In prison, Kendra is having a lot of conflict with the guards. She acts out, she disrespects them, and then she gets written up. Far too many disciplinary actions have been filed against her.

She starts fights with other inmates. She resents her cellmate to the point of sabotaging her things. Kendra puts little rips in her cellmate's pictures of her kids, pours water on her bed, hides her soap.

Kendra is acting out of frustration, of course, because she feels like a prisoner. She has no choices, no freedom, no escape, no possible change in her circumstances.

Kendra is focusing on what isn't working. She is stuck; she feels powerless. As a result, she acts out and contributes to the negative outcomes.

But is this actually true? Is she stuck, with no freedom, no choices?

No. She has a clear choice.

In his book *Interior Freedom*, Jacques Phillipe writes:

> "It is natural and easy to go along with pleasant situations that arise without our choosing them. It becomes a problem, obviously, when things are unpleasant, go against us, or make us suffer. But it is precisely then that, in order to become truly free, we are often called to choose to accept what we did not want…."

Frankl writes, "Everything can be taken from a man but one thing: the last of the human freedoms—to choose one's attitude in any given set of circumstances, to choose one's own way."

Solution-Focused Brief Therapy (SFBT)

Solution-Focused Brief Therapy (SFBT) focuses on strengths, on what is possible. The SFBT therapist is less concerned about what happened to you or how the problem came about. They care about solutions.

With Kendra, it isn't about her past. It isn't about the crimes that brought her to prison. It isn't about her current predicaments.

The problem is that she *feels* imprisoned. How can she find freedom?

The solution-focused therapist helps you see your own potential and focus on your own solutions. You are encouraged to focus on what you are doing to contribute to the problem. Then you use your strengths to find a solution.

This therapy is very empowering.

How do you want your life to be?

Isn't this the question at the heart of this whole book? "How do you want your life to be?"

Sit with that for a second. Maybe sit with it for a day. Maybe a week.

What is the problem?

The therapist will then ask, "What is the problem that needs addressing?" In other words, why is your life currently not how you want it to be?

This doesn't need to be a deep consideration of core thoughts or feelings. It's pretty surface.

You might say, I'm eating too much. I'm not fully engaged with my job. I am snapping at my kids a lot. I'm picking fights with my partner. I am checked out at my job, and I'm worried I'll get fired.

You know how you would answer this question. It is usually the first thought that comes to mind. But please remember, this isn't about the other person or the situation. You can't control the situation or the other person. What is the problem that *you* can fix?

We follow up with, "What will be different when this problem is solved?"

Dream about it for a minute. What would that look like? How would that feel?

What are the exceptions?
When was the problem less of a problem?

When do you *not* eat too much? When are you patient with your kids? When do you *not* pick a fight with your partner? When did you feel fully engaged with your work?

When was the problem less severe?

What did you do to contribute to that exception? When did you feel strong or competent or effective in that exception?

Is this a circumstance that you can recreate?

Solutions
Next, we focus on solutions. How do you get there? How do you accomplish this?

What are the things that must occur that can create that outcome? What steps must be taken? What needs to be done before you see your problem as solved?

With Kendra, we first explored "How do you want your life to be?"

Kendra couldn't change her circumstances, so she needed to explore her choices. She was in prison. These were the facts, and they could not change.

Frankl writes: "When we are no longer able to change a situation, we are challenged to change ourselves."

Once she accepted this, she could explore how to peacefully exist in the situation she found herself in. How did she want her life to be, if she was being forced to live it in prison?

Well, she admitted she was lonely. She had driven people away. She felt like she was unwanted. In fact, she felt like she was hated.

What she really wanted was to be accepted. She wanted friendships. She wanted to be sought out.

It turns out, that's who she used to be on the outside.

She had a great number of friends before incarceration. No matter where she had lived, her home was usually full of people. She took in strays. Her kids would bring home friends who would end up living there. Holidays were crowded in her house.

When we examined her strengths, it turns out she had a lot of social and interpersonal strengths. She made friends easily, and she was a caretaker. She had lost this part of herself in prison because she had been so busy reacting to her situation, a situation she could not change.

What would be different if she used those strengths to change her encounters with others here in prison? Could she envision a life on the inside where she had friends? Could people want to hang out with her? Could she open her heart and take care of others?

What is the most powerful thing Kendra can do?

She could use her strengths to find a solution.

Power isn't a fist or a hammer. Power is intentional behavior to solve a problem.

Sometimes the power doesn't need to affect your situation. It might be a powerful decision that affects your mental health.

"Forgive him"

For a bit of backstory, my mother was killed in a car crash when I was in my twenties. It was my father's birthday, and they had plans to go out to dinner that evening.

She was an artist, and she had completed a beautiful painting for his birthday gift. When we found it in her studio later that day, the varnish was still drying on the canvas.

The crash happened early that morning. She worked part time for the local newspaper and was driving to a nearby town. She had a cup of strong black coffee in the center console and a piece of buttered toast in her hand. She came to a stop at a stop sign on a quiet country road, waiting to cross a four-lane highway. No other cars were around.

As she began to proceed across the highway, a semi barreled around the curve towards her. He crossed four lanes of traffic and T-boned her van, shoving her into the far ditch.

The semi driver radioed for assistance, but my mother was beyond help. She had died on impact.

The back of his truck read "Guaranteed Overnight Delivery." It was 4:00 in the morning, and he was three hours away from a two-hour deadline.

He was in a rush. He was careless. He killed my mother. He destroyed our lives.

My dad loved my mom with his whole heart. He chuckled when she burned dinner. He teased that the smoke alarm was our dinner bell. He thought she was beautiful when she was angry. He drove around the block three times before embarking on a trip just to let her remember all the things she forgot to pack.

When she died, Dad was devastated. Shortly after her death, he died of a broken heart.

It was the truck drivers' fault that I'd lost them both. I was orphaned, and I blamed him.

I grew bitter. When I saw one of the trucks from that fleet, I'd give the driver the finger.

I became resentful of people who still had their moms. I wanted a dad to cheer me on. I was only in my twenties, way too young to be orphaned.

And it was all this guy's fault. If he hadn't been so rushed, if he hadn't been sleepy or distracted, he would have been more careful. He would have slowed down, he would have seen her van, he would have braked. She could have lived.

For years, I blamed this guy, and my resentment was toxic.

And then, one day I was teaching about feminist theory in my Counseling Theories class, and I posed the question to the students, "What is the most powerful thing you can do right now?"

Suddenly I knew my own answer.

Forgive him.

I didn't want to. He didn't deserve it. We never heard any apology from him.

But also, Anne Lamott says, "Not forgiving is like drinking rat poison and then waiting for the rat to die."

I had to forgive him. My refusal to forgive wasn't hurting him. It was hurting me.

What was the most powerful thing I could do right then, so many years after the crash?

On the anniversary of her death, my dad's birthday, I took the day off from work. I cancelled my classes. I brought my kids to school.

I made myself a cup of coffee, curled up on the sofa, and called the county highway patrol. I gave them the details of the crash and asked for the driver's name and phone number. It was all part of the public record.

I called him. He didn't pick up, thankfully, and I went to voice mail:

"Hi. You don't know me, but you were involved in a crash years ago. My mother was driving the van. I know what I am about to say has no bearing on your life whatsoever, but I need to say it out loud: I forgive you.

I am sad it happened. I am sad you were involved. I understand this accident probably had a terrible effect on you as well. I hope you can find forgiveness in your own life.

But for me, well, I needed to tell you, I forgive you."

I left my name again and gave him my number in case he wanted to call back. He never did.

What was the most powerful thing I could do that day? I forgave him.

I had to do it a bunch of days after that too. But it finally stuck. I have fully forgiven him.

It changed my life. It set me free.

Application

Now it's your turn. Breathe deeply and creatively reflect. Can you answer these questions in a way that will bring you the greatest amount of peace?

- How do you want your life to be?
- What is the problem you want changed?
- What will be different when it is solved?
- When was it less of a problem? When did it not exist?
- What are your strengths? Your skills? Where is your power?
- How can these be applied to your solution?
- What is the powerful thing you can do?
- How might you leave the greatest legacy?

9
PEOPLE
Who is in my corner?

Cast Away with Tom Hanks has one of the most emotionally moving moments in cinema history for me.

It was such a great movie. I was amazed that Hanks could carry most of the movie alone with no dialogue.

Well, there was a lot of one-sided dialogue between him and his quiet friend Wilson.

I really liked Wilson, with those big eyes and crooked smile. So easy-going. Rarely critical. Just a great companion.

Have you seen Wilson's studio headshot? Did you know Wilson is listed first and Tom Hanks is listed second in the movie cast on Wikipedia? Wilson even has an IMDB page.

If you haven't seen the movie, Wilson is a volleyball.

And when Wilson (spoiler alert) floats away from Chuck (Tom Hanks), I am heartbroken. To be honest, I am almost inconsolable.

Why do you think that is?

Because we are social animals. We are so desperate for human contact, we will anthropomorphize inanimate objects for companionship. Shoot, we project human traits onto our pets so that we feel less alone.

Don't we, Mittens? Who's a sweet kitten? Such a good girl!

Social Psychology

Yes, we are absolutely social creatures. In fact, I have some sad stories about this. Bear with me. I have a point.

There has been a lot of research on the impact of emotional deprivation in infants and children. Experiments on babies are never fun to read. But the results can give us really important information on development and attachment.

Failure to Thrive

Over 100 years ago, there were foundling hospitals in the US and the UK. Unwed mothers would leave their newborn infants there to be put up for adoption.

Nurses and nursing aids dressed in full PPE: caps, masks, gloves, gowns, aprons. They were instructed not to have any physical contact with the babies without protective gear. Skin-on-skin contact was forbidden. The reason for this was to reduce the possible transmission of viruses or bacteria. They didn't want to compromise the baby's health.

Staff were also instructed not to make eye contact with the babies. Visitors who were interested in adoption were requested not to touch the infants or make eye contact.

Making or maintaining eye contact posed a risk of the baby bonding with someone. Hospital leadership were concerned that if a baby bonded with an adult, this would impair the baby's ability to attach to the adoptive mother once the adoption took place.

Sadly, the mortality rate of these babies was high. In fact, it was significantly higher than infants raised in homes with mothers. Babies in the foundling hospitals, with their sterile conditions, died quickly. Babies raised at home, despite unsterile conditions (and very likely a lot of bacteria and viruses) survived.

Now, was this a question of quality of nutrition? Babies in the hospital were getting plenty of food, but not breast milk. But neither were adopted children. Adopted children still thrived.

Babies in the hospitals were in cribs most of the time. Were they perishing from limited mobility? Probably not. Babies in other environments where they were restricted (cradleboards, khangas, car seats) do not perish from being immobile. Besides, babies are not mobile on their own for at least the first six months of life.

Was the high mortality rate due to an impoverished play environment or lack of toys? Unlikely. Newborns and young babies tend not to have the small motor coordination to even use toys.

So, what caused this failure to thrive?

Attachment theorists concluded that babies died because they did not get the human touch and emotional contact they needed to survive. Physical touch and interpersonal contact are imperative.

We are a social species. The presence of other people is a basic human need. Without it, babies die.

Without it, adults die too.

Adult Socialization

I teach a module on suicide in my Psychopathology courses. One of the statistics that will usually surprise my students is the rate of completed suicides by state across the US.

Each year the state death rates are slightly different. Some years, the overall rates are higher; other years are lower. However, states with the highest rates are always the highest. The states with the lowest rates are always the lowest.

The states with the highest rates of completed suicides are consistently Montana, Alaska, Wyoming, New Mexico, Colorado, followed by states jockeying for position: Utah, South Dakota, Oklahoma, Idaho.

But what doesn't change are the states with the lowest rates of completed suicides: District of Columbia is always number one, followed by New York, New Jersey, Connecticut, California, and Illinois.

The states along the Atlantic are also protected, from Massachusetts to Maryland. There are significantly lower than average rates of completed suicides there.

Why do you think this is? What is so different between Montana and New Jersey? Well, besides terrain, food, culture, customs, politics, and horses?

The biggest difference is population density. The states with the *highest* rates of completed suicides have very low population density. The cities are smaller. The rural population is spread far apart. You are not packed tightly together. You are not surrounded by people. You don't see them unless you go looking.

The states with the *lowest* rates of completed suicides have cities with very dense populations. People are everywhere. You share apartment walls with them, you share seats with strangers on the train. You become accustomed to congested traffic and long checkout lines. While you might not like them, people seem to be everywhere.

The greater the population density, the lower the rates of completed suicide. Does this surprise you?

The presence of other people, even if you don't know them by name, will have a protective factor. We need other people. Without them, we die.

Impairments to Connection

I think this is part of the devastation of the COVID pandemic. While we had to protect ourselves and loved ones, sheltering in place isolated us. Not being able to commune with friends or family members who weren't living with us was really damaging.

Quarantining was especially harmful to our elderly who lived alone. Many of them didn't have access to technologies so they couldn't connect virtually. It caused them a failure to thrive.

Sheltering in place also harmed our children. They needed to relate to friends and classmates and develop social skills. Isolation impaired their social development.

I am seeing the consequences of this in the younger college students who are moving through my classrooms. This is a generation of kids who are less adept at collaborating, asking questions, or befriending strangers as students before the pandemic.

Screens

Another thing impairing children's ability to connect with us— and to one another—is the prevalence of screens. Two issues immediately leap to mind.

When a child is on a screen, their attention is hijacked. A toy is not designed to be as absorbing as a cartoon or video game.

A simple toy can allow the child to shift attention to whatever is most interesting.

When mommy is chatting with the barista, a child who isn't fixated on a screen will observe that social exchange. They will learn from watching the conversation that you can ask a question, listen to an answer, listen for a question, give an answer. Observing the adults helps the child learn how to have a conversation using the give and take of conversational dialogue.

Moreover, a child will observe other people engaging in and resolving conflict. Watching others, a child learns problem solving. They develop social scripts of how to live this complicated life.

But if a child is watching an engrossing, high-color, action-intense set of images, it pulls them in. They can't look away. As a result, that child misses out on a lot. Too much.

But the other problem that comes to mind what happens when the *parent* is on their screen.

The Still Face Experiment
In an experiment in 1975, Edward Tronick and fellow researchers conducted the Still Face Experiment.

The baby is strapped into a highchair or a bouncy seat in front of the mother. Mommy is instructed to connect with the baby.

Each mother very naturally connects with her infant. She is playful. She coos. She makes faces. She engages in singsong speech, mimics the baby's facial expression, makes silly sounds. You know how adorable that can get.

The videos show the baby lighting up, emoting brightly, copying mommy's sounds and facial expressions. The baby will point at something, and mommy follows with her eyes to see what baby is pointing at. She will cheerfully name and comment on it.

They coordinate their emotions and behaviors. There are a lot of mirror neurons firing on both sides. Super cute.

Then mommy is instructed by the researcher to look down and maintain a still face. Do not look at the baby, do not respond.

First, the baby continues to coo, gurgle, kick their chubby feet. They wave their chunky little hands with those tiny dimples where knuckles are supposed to be. The baby points at something they see in order to direct mommy's gaze.

No response from mommy.

That baby tries even harder to get mommy's attention. They escalate in cuteness. They crank it to eleven. They sigh happily, growl playfully. They roar loudly. They laugh.

Baby looks intently at mommy's blank face and coos louder. Baby does more of the imitations of mommy's original sing-song sounds and expressions.

But mommy continues to look downward, emotionless. Her face expressionless.

Now baby grows noticeably agitated.

Baby fights against this situation: wriggling, struggling, kicking their feet out in front of them in frustration. They screech to alert mommy that this is not going well at all! Baby may even cry, wail, or howl.

When all of baby's attempts for connection fail, the baby withdraws. They turn away from mommy in their little bouncy seat. The previously excited, animated baby face morphs into a withdrawn, hopeless expression.

Whenever I see video replications of this study, I find it distressing. I feel so sad for the baby.

And I am astounded by how much the mommy looks like she is on her phone.

Bids for Connection

John Gottman is my favorite marriage researcher. He has been researching marriage for almost as long as I've been alive. Don't tell him I said that.

He studies couples as they fight, as they forgive, as they repair the tears in the relationship, and especially how couples connect. If you are married, I encourage you to read all things Gottman.

This is my favorite though. Gottman encourages you to recognize your attempts to connect with one another. That baby, with all the coos and gurgles and cuteness, was making *bids* for mommy's attention.

You do this with your partner, too. You just don't do it by screeching, gurgling spit, and kicking your feet out in front of you.

Well, maybe you do. I don't know. You can be weird like that.

Your bids in romantic relationships are usually much more subtle. I make a bid for my husband's attention by kissing him on the top of the head when he's sitting at his desk. He throws out a bid by tugging playfully on my hair.

Just like the baby in the still face experiment, you make bids for another's attention. But the connection doesn't happen on your end when you make the bid. The connection happens when the other person responds.

Here is a classic Gottman example: you look out the window and say, "There's a bird out here." This is a neutral, potentially boring observation.

Turning away

Your partner can respond in one of three ways. They can *turn away* from the bid. They leave it hanging, without comment. They look at their phone or they say something completely unrelated to the bird. Maybe they are distracted. Maybe they didn't hear you. A connection is not made.

Turning against

Your partner can *turn against* the bid. "What do I care?" Turning against might be an eye roll, an annoyed sigh. Turning against a bid isn't always aggressive, but it can feel like your attempt is being swatted away.

Turning Towards

The third, and preferred, option is to *turn towards* the bid. Ask, "A bird?" "What color is it?" or "Is it tweeting?" You can come to the window and look at the bird with your partner. You can say, "That reminds me. Should we have squab for dinner?"

Turning toward the bid is simple. It takes only a few seconds to pay attention to your partner's little, subtle attempt at connection.

When I talk about this in class, we usually discover that many bids are physical or humorous. Your partner will bid for connection with a joke, a flirt, a wink, a poke, a tickle, or a pat on the butt.

When I ask the how they usually turn towards that bid, students are not quite sure. But when they come back from small group discussions, they admit that it doesn't take much: a smile, a giggle, a wink in response. Patting the other person's butt is always a good option.

How hard is it to smile when your person tries to connect with you? Eye contact and a smile is all it takes to reassure them that you are with them. You are on their side. Turning towards those bids will create a strong connection.

John Gottman says so.

We are social animals, and we crave connection with others. But without the presence of others, we perish—babies and adults alike.

Abraham Maslow, in his theory of the hierarchy of needs, believed that you have a deep need for love and belonging. If you are meeting your physical needs of food, water, and shelter, and if you are physically safe, then you need to belong to someone. You need to be significant to at least one other person.

William Glasser agreed. We need satisfying relationships.

Nurturing Relationships

Who are your people? Who do you turn towards? Who is in your corner?

The presence of others is good. But the presence of others who support you is better.

And they are imperative for good mental health.

A few months after Scott died, I was driving my daughter to a modeling shoot. It was the day after Christmas; the roads were really slick, and she didn't want to drive herself.

Sleet hit the windshield, icing it up on contact. Cars were sliding off the roads to our right and to our left. We made it to the shoot, she posed all the different angular ways they make one do, and then we climbed back into the car to drive home.

The snow was accumulating on top of the ice. The roads were not only slippery, but it was also hard to tell where the lanes were. The ditches looked the same height as the breakdown lanes. We drove at a snail's pace.

And yet, we hit a particularly icy patch, spun around on the freeway, and ended up backwards in the ditch, snow up to the top of the wheel wells.

I called roadside assistance, and they told me they were really overwhelmed with the storm so it would be a couple hours. They told me to just leave the keys in the car and suggested we find a ride home. They would call me when the car was back at the garage.

Great.

Who could I call to come get us? As his wife, I would have called Scott. As a widow, I was at a loss. Who would venture out into the middle of a snowstorm in perilous driving conditions?

I made a few calls, but no help came. My brother had just taken his son and his friends to see a movie at the theater and couldn't leave them unchaperoned. My sister-in-law was interviewing a new hire. Scott's best friend didn't answer. My best friend was out of town. There was no one else. My parents were gone, my other siblings far away. Scott's larger family was equally suffering.

It was in that moment I realized something. When Scott was alive, I had dedicated most of my social time to my little family. I hadn't really nurtured friendships with other people. I guess I didn't think I needed to.

But here my daughter and I sat, in a stalled car, in the ditch, no heater, the cold starting to cut through to the bone. I needed to figure this out.

Thankfully, I remembered someone! She had asked at the funeral how she could help. I called her and she answered her phone. She had an all-wheel drive SUV, and she grew up in Iowa, so she knew what to do.

She was so kind to us when we got into her warm car with the heated seats. She drove us safely home. She even thanked me for calling her and asking for her help!

But this was a wake-up call for me. Marriage and kids had just consumed my time and I hadn't prioritized friendships. But my isolation had become tangibly painful in my grief. When it occurred to me that I didn't even have someone to call in a moment of crisis, I had to make some changes.

So, I have been intentional in fostering relationships that are good for my mental health.

When I am struggling, stressed, afraid, or sad, I know immediately who I need to call. When I'm excited, celebrating a victory, proud of how I've overcome something hard, I know who to call. These people are in my favorites list on my phone, just below my kids and just above my hairdresser.

Along with immediate family, who is on your list when you are in crisis? Who do you call when you need to celebrate? Are they the same people?

I have a group of friends that help me navigate the insanity of academia. I have a group of friends who see patients and understand my horror stories. I have a small group of friends who are professional speakers, and we help each other figure out some of the challenges of the job.

Who are your work friends who share your common stories? Did you know that people with close friends at work rate
their lives as happier? They aren't just happier at work. Their
lives are happier. They have overall greater well-being.

I have a small group of friends that hold me accountable in
my faith and who engage with me in deeper spiritual and existential questions. I have friends who are married, and we go out
to dinner as couples. Our neighbors get together for backyard
firepits a couple times a year where we talk about homeowner
woes.

Who are the friends you purposefully call for companionship and conversation? Are you engaging in social connections
outside of work and family? Are you nurturing those relationships regularly?

Research shows that we are more likely to make healthy
choices and have better physical and mental health when we are
socially connected. Your friends' health habits tend to influence
your own health habits. You are less likely to be sedentary when
your friends are all active. You are more likely to exercise. You
are more likely to engage in spiritual disciplines when your
friends do. You are less likely to smoke if your friends don't
smoke. You are less likely to drink to excess if your friends only
drink in moderation. You get the picture.

You are also better at coping with hard times when you have
stable and supportive relationships. When you have strong
friendships, you are more resilient against stress, anxiety, and depression as well.

Friendships are good for your work health, for your physical
health, and they are definitely good for your mental health.

Application

Take a moment and consider the people you love and who love you. Consider the ones who may require some boundaries.

- Who is in your corner?
- Who do you call when you are in crisis?
- Who cheers you on when you are doing well?
- How are you engaging in social connections outside of work and family?
- Who is not so healthy to be around?
  - How can you set boundaries around those relationships?
  - What parts of those relationships do you need to avoid?
- How can you nurture your healthiest relationships?
- Who has been good for your mental health?
  - Can you spend more time with them?

10
PLAN
What is my Goal?

As I've been writing this to you, my first question was about purpose, and we both decided you were an existentialist.

My second question asked about your passions: your needs and wants.

My third question asked you about presence. What are you aware of right now? We chatted about the plot of your personal narrative. We took a pretty deep dive into your perspective and what you say to yourself. We agreed perfectionism is toxic and post-traumatic growth is possible. Then we located your power. Just now, you named your people.

Now it's time to make a plan.

To enhance your personal functioning, you want to respond to your life, not react to it. Good mental health requires intention and attention; it needs direction and focus. Wishing is not sufficient. Insight isn't enough.

The reason I didn't use Freud's theories in any of the modules is because he didn't have any strategies for improvement.

He listened to his patients, looking for themes. Then, in his Austrian accent, he'd day: "I vunder if your neurosis iz due to cunflikts vis your muzzer."

Well, duh, Sigmund. Of course, it is my mother's fault. But what do I do about that *now*? You see, Freud didn't offer solutions. He didn't encourage momentum. He didn't discuss change. He didn't focus on goals. He didn't assign tasks.

Viktor Frankl, in *Man's Search for Meaning*, writes,

"I consider it a dangerous misconception of mental hygiene to assume that what man needs in the first place is equilibrium or, as it is called in biology 'homeostasis', i.e., a tensionless state. What man actually needs is not a tensionless state but rather the striving and struggling for a worthwhile goal, a freely chosen task."

I am giving you a template to develop greater mental health hygiene. You have the tools you need. You have ten psychological theories that work. These theories have been clinically proven and scientifically researched.

From those theories, you have questions that guide you. They isolate the most relevant points of each theory to apply to your life.

Your responses to the questions provide a current record of your personal functioning. I hope you cultivated some self-compassion. You have established some clarity of thought. You've become aware of your emotions.

Through this process, you have developed greater self - awareness. You have a created a clearer sense of where you are strong. You can also see where you can develop more skills.

Now let's pull it all together and set a goal. Setting and accomplishing goals is good mental health.

The Plan

Early on, I said we have limited days, and we don't know how many more there will be. I mentioned the epitaph, and that your life is just a dash on the tombstone.

I admitted to you one of my biggest regrets. As a mother, I prioritized cleanliness over my relationship with my little family.

I could have made memories with them. Instead, I shooed them out the door and scrubbed away all evidence they existed.

While this is a deep regret, I can't do anything to change it. The only think I can do is accept is as the past and now work to be different. My kids are older, and although Scott is gone, the three of us can choose to enjoy our time together.

Now my house is not pristine, and I've decided not to care. I've stopped living under the tyranny of a dead (and possibly mentally ill) grandmother.

And my mess is not a health hazard or anything, but I will need to swish the toilets a bit before I let you in.

Regret

Questions around regret may be painful to consider. Regret holds so much guilt, shame, and remorse. Those are painful. But that's okay. Fleeing from those feelings and running from your regrets don't move you forward. They keep you stuck in the same behaviors because you're pretending you can't control them.

Guilt, shame, remorse. Those are hard. It's okay. We can sit with that distress for a little bit. Take a deep breath; close your eyes. Reflect on this question:

What do you regret?

Here is another question that may feel a bit more empowering: If you continue on this current path, when you look back a year from now, what will you regret not changing?

Your answers tell you what you value compared to what you *thought* you valued in that moment.

I thought I valued a clean house, but that got in the way of what I really valued: time with my kids. When I would fight with my husband, I thought my opinions really mattered. Looking back, I regret fighting over ideas because, turns out, what I really loved was him.

Look at your regrets. What do they tell you about what you value most?

On the flip side, and way more fun to answer, is the question, "What are you grateful for?"

We talked about gratitude in an earlier chapter, and I still hold that it is a game changer. The value of gratitude in this context is that you can see even clearer patterns that point you to what you value.

I am inviting you to set a true, authentic, and meaningful goal for good mental health. To do that, we need to tap into what is most important to you.

What do you regret, and what might you regret if you don't make a change? The pain of a failed attempt, a risk gone wrong, is temporary. You move on. You learn from it. You try again. The pain of regret can feel permanent.

Hope

What is your hope?

When my speaking coach told me a couple years ago that I should write and speak about hope, I wrinkled my nose in distaste.

I shook my head. "No."

She seemed shocked! "Why not?"

"Because," I explained, "hope is nothing but rainbows and feathers and butterfly wings. It's calligraphy on wall hangings. It doesn't mean anything. It's so, so…ephemeral. There's nothing there."

You see, I thought hope was insubstantial.

And then, when I stood in the Emergency Room as my child described his imminent death to a stranger, I realized hope is the most substantial thing in the world.

Without hope, my child almost died.

So I launched hard into a long study on hope. This is what professors do when they are scared: they research the heck out of the problem.

It turns out hope is *not* rainbows and feathers and butterfly wings.

Hope is optimism with teeth.

Hope is setting out a goal and making a plan. It is recognizing what you can control, even in the face of desperation and chaos. Hope is taking control of what you can; it's turning your strengths into a strategy.

There was a hope study conducted in China a few years ago. I can't find it anywhere right now so I can't reference it. I really hope I didn't hallucinate the whole thing in one of those vivid dreams.

This is also something university professors do—dream up entire research projects and believe they are real.

Anyway, in this study, researchers interviewed terminally ill patients with limited time left and asked them what they hoped for.

Interesting! Right? If you think so, that's the existentialist in you.

In the interview, the researcher first asked the patient to reflect on a specific event:

"Think about a time when you set a goal for yourself, created a plan, and followed the plan to completion and accomplished the goal."

"What was the goal?"

"What was the plan?"

"What steps did you follow?"

"What were your obstacles?"

"How did you feel when you accomplished your goal?"

Then the patents were asked to rate their level of hopefulness. Next, they were asked to identify something they hoped for related to their imminent death.

Beautiful hopes sprung up: I hope for my adult children to reconcile. I hope for my family to be by my side. I hope for a good death.

For the next phase, each patient identified the steps they needed to take to accomplish this goal. They were invited to be as detailed as possible.

Steps may have included inviting each adult child individually to the home to discuss one's dying wish. Perhaps the patient needed to speak with physicians about medications. Was there something that could ease their pain yet leave them cogent enough to talk with loved ones as they neared the end?

Specifically, each patient focused on what they could plan for, what they could control.

At the end of the study, participants were asked if they had hope in their death. Each one responded with "yes."

In Mandarin, of course.

Hope is optimism with a plan.

I invite you to do this for yourself. Think about a time you set a goal for yourself and you met it. Maybe it was to learn a recipe. Play an instrument. Maybe it was to overcome a fear. Was it to paint your living room? To run a marathon?

What was the goal? What steps did you set out for yourself? What were the obstacles? How did you feel when you accomplished your goal?

Whatever the goal may have been, you were able to attain it. And this is evidence that you can attain other goals as well.

Now let's consider what kind of goal you can set now. Specifically, how might your goal help your mental health?

First, let's think about what you might want to tackle. Do you recall from the questions in the introduction? If you went to bed tonight and a miracle occurred, but you didn't realize a miracle was happening while you were asleep, what would be the miracle? And what would be the first indication tomorrow morning that a miracle had occurred?

To set a goal, ask yourself, how do you want your life to be?

The answer tells you about a need that has been going unmet. There is a value that isn't being satisfied.

Your first response might be surface level. "I want to be thin." But what is the need that lies beneath it? What will thinness bring you? Respect from others? Approval from "them"? Are you looking for self-acceptance? Confidence? Does being thin give you boldness or courage? What is the deeper craving that underlies thinness?

"I want enough money so I can buy anything I want." Are you craving things, or are you craving security? Do you want what money can buy, or do you want respect that money represents? Are you searching for a piece of the pie, or do you really want peace of mind? What is the deeper need that money will meet?

I wanted to be a psychologist. I thought it was because it offered a fun and funny lifestyle in a condo overlooking the city.

But it turns out what I really desired was meaningful work. I craved deep connections with other people in a safe and intimate setting. Now I live in a suburban house full of harps and scuba gear.

 What is your hope?

How do you want your life to be? What need do you want to meet?

If you are pretty sure of one thing you need, can you imagine how life will be different when you meet it?

This can lead you to the next answer: What is one goal to focus on right now?

The SMART Goal

The first step in setting a goal is to decide.

There is an acronym in Goal Setting Theory called SMART goals.

Specific

A smart goal is *specific*. There is no ambiguity or misinterpretation or wiggle-room. Saying "I want to be happy" is not as precise and detailed as "I want to be content in my own home whenever I am here. Specifically, I want to feel calmness in my chest when I walk through the door."

Measurable

A SMART goal is *measurable*. Can you track your progress by days? By dollars? By every time you engage in the new habit? You need to know when you've reached the finish line and accomplished the goal.

To write this book, I set a deadline for myself that was clear and practical. I set a date that I would have the first draft done. I put it on my calendar.

In fact, if I didn't have it done by that exact date, I promised myself I would pay my coach $350 for nothing—no coaching, no conversation. I would get nothing from her, and she would get no explanation from me. She would just get a nice fat check.

And I absolutely did not want to do that! I can't afford $350 for nothing! But I had a deadline, and now I needed to keep it.

How was I going to measure my progress toward that deadline? I couldn't just wish it to happen, every day bringing a harbinger of doom while I actively ignored my closed laptop. The goal was measurable, and the steps needed to be measurable too.

I committed to using the Pomodoro technique: focus for 25 minutes, take a five-minute break, and repeat. If I did this four times (usually in a row), I could write at least 100 minutes every day. My consequences if I didn't: disgust, shame, and self-loathing.

I also promised myself a reward each day if I met that 100-minute mark. That reward was a bag of blue Nerds Clusters at the end of the day.

Don't judge me. Have you tried them? They're like crack.

Achievable

Achievable goals are the only kind to set. Is your goal realistic? Is it doable? Will this goal require determination but not herculean effort? Is this goal something you're likely to do? Is the goal something that you might enjoy doing? Can you make it entertaining? We are most likely to accomplish goals that contain an element of fun.

To reach my deadline, I needed to break my goal down into 100-minute chunks because I knew I could not carve out more time than that.

You see, I am quite busy. I teach full time; I see patients part time. I host a podcast. I teach overload courses for a graduate program. I am newly married, and I am parenting an adolescent child through a mental illness.

While it felt unrealistic for me to even attempt this, the need to write the book was pressing so hard on my mind that I had to do it. It was a huge priority. I knew that writing this book would be good for my own mental health. I also knew that it was urgent that I write it for you.

Man, I hope this is helping you.

Unfortunately, if you are like me, when you reach a goal, you don't celebrate it. You refuse to acknowledge it. You may even punish yourself with disgust, shame, and self-loathing.

And then, if you are like me, you push the goal further out.

Me: "I wrote for two hours today!"

Also me: "Yeah? Well, you could have written for two *more* hours, but you wasted time lying around. You came home from work, and you ate candy and drank wine and took a bath and listened to true crime podcasts. You screwed it all up."

Don't be like me. Don't push your goals further out and then punish yourself for not meeting them. Don't extend them to the point of being unreachable and then dump disgust, shame, and self-loathing on your head. You never even set those impossible goals for yourself in the first place. They were your afterthought, all for the sake of being cruel.

Make achievable goals, reach them, and then celebrate.

I think I might try this tonight.

Me: "I wrote for two hours today!"

Me: "YAY!! Let me pour you some wine! Boxed okay? I'm running you a bath. Have some Nerds Clusters! Here's Keith Morrison on *Dateline*!! By the way, you're going to do this again tomorrow. You're doing great!"

Relevant

A SMART goal is *relevant*.

Earlier I asked what goal you might set, and what is the deeper need you would like to meet?

Focus on that again for a bit.

Let's say your partner works from home and they let their dishes pile up in the sink throughout the day. You come home after a long day and an endless commute, and what's the first thing you see? Dirty dishes in the sink.

You feel disrespected. You feel undervalued. You feel dismissed. And underneath it all, you feel disconnected. You love them, but—in the moment—you don't feel loved back.

Now, as you imagine the scenario, what do you need in that moment? (Don't say a clean sink.) Do you need respect? To be valued? To be seen? To feel connected?

When you can isolate what it is you really need, then you can make some decisions about behaviors that will help meet your need.

What is the most powerful thing you can do right now?

Is yelling the most powerful thing you can do? Can slamming cupboard doors let them know you're upset? How about breaking a few dishes? Put a chip in their favorite coffee mug?

What will that get you?

Attempting to manipulate or control their behavior will not accomplish your goal. It will harm them, harm you, and even harm your relationship. Robert Heinlein's character Lazarus Long said, "Never attempt to teach a pig to sing; it wastes your time and annoys the pig."

No, I am not calling your partner a pig. I am telling you that you cannot change someone else; you cannot make them do something that is not in their nature.

You can't control anyone else's behavior. The only behavior you can control is your own.

I know. That truth is harsh. The sooner you learn it, the more peaceful your life will be. The lives of the people around you will be more peaceful too.

Instead of yelling, slamming, breaking things, look at what has worked before. What was more powerful than a tantrum?

When *have* you felt respected, valued, seen? When have you felt connected to your partner?

What did you do to contribute to that? If you can see what you've done well in the past, can you do more of that?

So, what works? A deep breath? A smile? An invitation: "Hey, want to hang out with me in the kitchen? I'll put away groceries while you clean up the dishes. You pick the music; I'll dance with you!"

Maybe they aren't receptive to that. Maybe that kind of invitation is usually rebuffed. Perhaps you feel too vulnerable at the end of the day to put yourself out there like that. Maybe you're too tired to even think of a way to invite them in. I get it.

Your goal may be to find ways to self-soothe and take care of yourself. Your ultimate goal is to find some internal peace.

Perhaps your relevant goal is to walk into the house and go into the bedroom where you can decompress and meditate for ten minutes. You can completely redirect your focus. Your relationship with your self will matter more and the dishes will matter less.

Make your goal relevant to your need. See if you can tie them together.

Time-bound

Finally, a SMART goal is *time-bound*. You need a timeline that will indicate to you that you have achieved it—not with perfection but with slow and steady progress.

How much time will you need to accomplish this goal? Make a reasonable due date that can allow for some error but is also certain and clear. Look at your calendar and pick the day you want this done.

When you reach your deadline, then assess how far you have come and where you can go next. You can even set a new SMART goal to get you to the next level.

Let's use my example of writing this book through the lens of the SMART Goal components, and then we will do yours.

Need: I need to write a book. I can't waste any more time.

Goal: Write a book in six weeks

SMART Goal:

✓ I will write first draft of a book on mental health (*specific*).

✓ I will write for at least 100 minutes a day, every day (*measurable*).

✓ I will carve out time on my calendar each day. I will set my butt in the chair, I will open my laptop, and I will get my music going in the background. I will set a timer for 25 minutes, and I will write. When the alarm sounds, I will take a five-minute break, and repeat (*achievable*).

✓ Writing every day will develop a habit that gets me incrementally closer to my goal (*relevant*)…

✓ of having the book completed in six weeks (*time-bound*).

Perhaps you have always wanted to go to college. Let's make this a reality by setting out a SMART goal. "I want to finish college" is your driving motivation. What's the need that lies at the base of it? Do you need to do this to enhance your self-esteem? You know you are smart, and it's time to prove it to yourself? You need to learn about something so you can get the job that fits your personality and ideal work style?

The SMART goal is one incremental step toward finishing the bigger one. "I want to get my college degree" will start with a goal:

✓ Specific (I will research colleges in my area and online.)

✓ Measurable (I'll record the information on a graph).

✓ Achievable (I can do this over lunch every day).

✓ Relevant (I want to compare their programs: what they offer, the cost, their student aid packages, the length of the programs, etc.)

✓ Time-Bound (I will have information on ten colleges completed by a week from Friday).

Then you reassess, set a new SMART goal, and start again to move you even closer to your end goal. You get the gist.

Your Turn

What do you need? What goal can you set right now to move yourself toward better mental health?

- ✓ Specific (What will I do?)
- ✓ Measurable (How can I consistently measure it?)
- ✓ Achievable (Is it realistic?)
- ✓ Relevant (How does this goal directly relate back to a need?)
- ✓ Time-Bound (When do I want to have this accomplished? What is my deadline?)

Please remember that perfectionism is *not* the goal. Progress over perfection.

By the way, as I am writing this, I will confess that I did not write a word this past weekend other than an occasional text of "Where are you?" and "We're heading to the restaurant" and "My hotel key stopped working."

I allowed myself exceptions to the measurable part of "I will write every day." I was at a family reunion with people I rarely see. I wanted to pour all my energy and attention into connecting with loved ones.

But did I beat myself up for not writing? No, because I was doing something else that I valued highly. I knew this was a worthy exception.

If I had skipped writing because I didn't feel it or because I'd lost momentum, I would reassess my goal and see if maybe I had set it too high; maybe it was unachievable.

You set a goal to start your business on Etsy. But then you don't check the orders for two days. Why? Well, both kids have the stomach flu. The dog has diarrhea. The cat needs surgery to remove a rubber tip that he bit off a nerf dart and it is obstructing his small intestine.

Oddly specific reason, you say?

He was fine until they had to reopen the incision four days later because he'd eaten a second one.

Then I wanted to kill him.

Give yourself a little grace when the routine you set out for yourself doesn't happen.

Consistency is key, of course, but exceptions may be necessary. When you find there are too many exceptions, and you are not moving towards the goal at the rate you had hoped, you may need to re-evaluate.

In setting a goal, you can explore, "What tends to stop me?" What causes me to give up? What is my most common setback? What usually sabotages my efforts? What makes me forfeit the goal altogether?

Behavior Therapy

If there is a behavior that sabotages you, we may need to call it out. Once you identify it, you can explore the underlying need that behavior is attempting to meet.

That unwanted behavior is doing something for you. It is serving a purpose. When you figure out what that is, then you can replace it with something else that meets that same need.

Remember I told you I had an undiagnosed, untreated illness that took me from the stage? I ended up homeless because of it. When I finally made it back to Minnesota, I went to the Mayo Clinic and received a diagnosis. The illness turned out to be a serious autoimmune disorder.

This brought me down a path of numerous treatments that didn't work. I tried a series of serious medications with severe side effects. The most bothersome side effect for me was significant weight gain.

There was a particular medication that I used to manage flares. It was the only thing that worked enough for me to function. The problem was the medication caused intense cravings and slowed down my metabolism.

Great combination. I wanted to eat entire loaves of bread that went directly to my thighs.

Years later, my doctor prescribed a form of chemotherapy, a tumor necrosis factor protein, that worked for me. In fact, it sent me into remission. I was doing so much better, but now I was morbidly obese.

A serious heart event scared me, and my lovely cardiologist told me I had to lose 100 pounds. He said I had no choice.

For my first attempt to lose weight, I decided to restrict calories all day, and when I'd get home in the evening I could eat a normal meal. This could have potentially worked. People lose weight on intermittent fasting quite effectively.

Except I ate a few calories throughout the day. I was restricting myself to cream and sugar in my coffee. Half a granola bar. A handful of peanut M&Ms. Then I would come home, eat dinner, then consume every snack I could find in the kitchen.

The caloric deprivation during the day triggered binges at night.

And then I watched a documentary on sumo wrestlers.

Your response to this is, ".... why?"

Anyway, here is what I learned. Sumo wrestlers are chunky fellas. The bigger, the better. They purposefully try to put on weight.

They do this by restricting calories all day while training, and then they eat massive amounts of calories before bed.

Are you picking up what I'm putting down here?

I was on the Sumo Wrestlers Diet! All I needed was the topknot.

I went to a dietician who shook her head, "When you do this, you are destroying your metabolism. You are throwing wet logs on a smoldering fire. There's no way your body can burn calories efficiently."

To reach my goal of better health and a stronger heart, there were behavioral changes I had to make. I couldn't just wish for better health. And I couldn't be a sumo wrestler.

Changing a Behavior

During a past semester, some of my psychology students were frustrated with another professor. They found his lectures, which he read from the podium in a monotone voice to be, well, boring.

They knew he was an interesting guy. He was an expert in his field, for goodness' sake! And he could be funny when he wasn't reading his lecture notes.

So they decided they needed to get him away from his notes and the podium. Their goal: train Dr. X to teach from the doorway every class period.

It was a small class. They talked to the other students and explained what they wanted to do. Everyone agreed to join in.

First, the students identified what this professor found reinforcing. Like all professors, he liked when students took notes, acted interested, laughed at his jokes.

To begin, every time Professor X approached the right side of the podium, the students leaned forward. They acted enthralled. Some nodded and smiled; others took notes.

When the professor moved back to the center of the podium, students acted bored. Some would relax their posture, stare out the window. Others would pick at their nails, check the clock behind them, or gaze at the ceiling. Someone would sigh heavily.

The following week, if he moved completely away from behind the podium, they would eagerly pay attention. When he moved back behind the podium at all, they'd quickly lose interest.

The next week, one student got to class early, put a small mark at the top of the whiteboard for all the students to see. If Professor X moved past the mark, the students leaned in. Back to the podium? Bored.

Week by week, they moved the mark on the top of the whiteboard closer to the doorway. Professor X learned to hover further and further to the right side of the room.

Students continued shaping his behavior each class period. The were interested only when he was within five feet of the door. Then within arm's reach of the door. Then when he stood by the door.

You guessed it.

Through cooperation of the students shaping his behavior, Dr. X taught more than 75% of each lecture leaning against the door frame!

He never realized what had happened. I asked him during finals week how his classes had gone over the semester.

He said his 2 PM class was amazing. He thought that group of students were particularly dynamic. Smartest group of kids he'd ever taught.

This tenured professor with his fancy doctorate had no idea his college sophomores had trained him like a lab rat.

Reinforcement

There are some effective ways to change your behavior too. You don't need others to help you. It all comes down to figuring out what your reward is. What is immediately reinforcing?

When you are doing something you wish you wouldn't, take a step back and ask, "What do I get out of doing that?" In other words, what is the payoff?

Are you yelling at your kids a lot? What's the payoff? Do they jump to it and do what you want?

If we know what is reinforcing the behavior, then we can figure out a different way of getting that same need met.

My son's preschool teacher was exasperated one day when I went to pick him up. She asked if she could get my advice on something.

A new boy was dropping the f-bomb. A lot. All day long she'd hear the effenheimer spurting out of this 3-year-old's mouth.

She didn't know what to do. She'd asked him to stop; she'd put him in time out. She exhausted all of her resources, and he was using it even more.

Using the train-your-professor technique from my college students, we discussed a different option.

What was the need being met by dropping the f-bomb? Little dude was getting attention from the teacher.

No, it wasn't high praise, but it was something. He was also using the word as an exclamation of frustration or when he was upset.

What did Susan want instead? She wanted him to use a different word.

We planned it out. The next morning, as soon as he dropped the first expletive of the day, Susan raced over to him.

"Oh, honey, we don't use that word here. None of the other kids say it. When we get frustrated in Miss Susan's room, we say 'quad.' Can you say that?"

Little man hesitated, worked his little mouth around it, and said, "Quad?"

She jumped back, acting slightly startled. "That's a very big word. We only use it when we have very big feelings. Watch."

She set up a small stack of blocks, and with his big eyes on her, she knocked the tiny tower over. Then she balled up her fists and exploded with "QUAD!"

Then she asked him to try it. She stacked the tower of blocks again, asked him if he was ready, and then she knocked the tower down.

Hesitantly, he said, "Quad?"

She gushed, "You sound really upset! Are you okay?"

He gravely nodded.

She reminded him, "We only use it when we are very upset, though, okay?"

He nodded, understanding this completely.

Within ten seconds of her walking away, she heard a little dude yelling, "QUAD!"

She raced back, knelt down, gave him all of her attention. Checked in with him. Made sure he was fine.

Over and over, all morning, she was rushing to this little guy's aid. Minor infractions and little frustrations were all punctuated with loud "quad" bombs.

Guess what word she never heard in that classroom again. The F-bomb

The value of this strategy was that she didn't ask him to stop something. She simply replaced it with something else. The universe abhors a vacuum. We can't stop an unwanted behavior without backfilling it with another one.

To stop an undesired behavior, it's imperative you replace it with a more desirable one. But the reward needs to be there. The payoff is what you were seeking this whole time. The new behavior will have to be just as rewarding to you as the old one.

Are you yelling at your kids a lot because it relieves your frustration and other hard emotions? Ask yourself how else you can accomplish this? Exercise? More sleep? Journaling? Discussing it with someone who makes you laugh?

To change a behavior, you can choose something else that you are already very likely to do. Instead of binge eating in front of the TV, pick up your crochet hook or something else to occupy your hands.

I was obese and the doctor told me to fix it. There was a bit of a problem though. I used to say, "I will do anything to lose weight… except diet and exercise."

Guess what I had to do?

The diet was a commitment. It was hard; it took effort. I set out SMART goals. I worked on reducing my binges and eating better throughout the day.

Slowly (very slowly) it became a habit, and I found it intrinsically rewarding to see the scale go down and the wardrobe get loose. There were discouraging plateaus, but I had a support group and a dietician who helped me through the stalls.

The diet was hard, but exercise was harder.

I don't like doing it. I don't like to sweat. I don't know how to swim. I've never been one of those people who enjoys getting out of a chair.

But I had to strengthen my heart. That was the whole point of this. Exercise had to be part of my health regimen.

How could I make this pleasant? What could I use to reinforce my changes?

To start, I recognized what my favorite things are: coffee and shoes. Coffee is my primary form of hydration.

And shoes?

Oh! I am an avid shoe wearer.

I wear shoes a lot. Often outside. I would say I wear shoes almost every day. I always wear shoes when I go to the store. To church. To dinner. It's guaranteed I will always wear a pair of shoes to work and keep them on throughout most of the morning.

Shoes are great!

I love coffee. I love shoes. What if I could pair these two things together to start exercising?

Every night, as I was doing my nightly shutdown routine, I put my tennis shoes on top of the coffee maker. The next morning, I'd wake up, stumble into the kitchen in my pajamas and socks, but before I could make the coffee, I had to move the shoes off the coffee maker.

Well, since they were in my hand, I might as well put them on.

Then I'd be standing there, in my pajamas and tennis shoes, waiting for the coffee to brew.

Well, this is silly! I might as well walk on the treadmill for ten minutes while the coffee is brewing.

After two weeks of consistent walking, I rewarded myself with a different coffee maker. At the thrift store I found a coffee machine with a burr grinder and thermal carafe. I still love that thing.

With this new coffee maker, coffee took longer to brew, and it was even more delicious. Since the longer grind and brew time and the thermal carafe gave me more time, I went farther distances on the treadmill.

After two more weeks of consistent walking and increased distances, I bought myself a new pair of tennis shoes.

Every ten pounds lost, I rewarded myself with something I could wear that was not dependent on my dress size. What could that be?

Shoes!

If I hit a plateau that lasted more than a week, I needed encouragement. So, I'd get a different coffee maker from the thrift store.

I now have four brewing systems and two espresso machines. I have owned drip coffee makers, single cup brewing systems, a French press, an AeroPress, a glass coffee funnel, a percolator, a Moka pot, Turkish coffee pot, a Beehouse dripper, a Vietnamese dripper, and a cold brew cask.

I'm sure I've left a few out. I hit a lot of plateaus.

I knew what I wanted to accomplish. I knew the behaviors that I needed to replace and the behaviors I needed to develop to get there. I used strong reinforcements, including social support and accountability, to achieve it. It was the hardest thing I've ever done.

For ten years now, I am 105 pounds down. I am highly caffeinated, and you should see all my shoes!

Setting goals to create long-term change is difficult. I would never suggest it was easy.

Viktor Frankl wrote, "What man actually needs is not a tensionless state but rather the striving and struggling for some goal worthy of him."

You are worthy of the struggle. It will bring you to better mental health.

Application

Stop reading for a minute and take a couple breaths. You've read a lot of information and answered a of questions. Now go back over your past answers and start making a plan.

- What behavior do you want to change? What need were you trying to meet?
- What is sustaining the current behavior? What is the payoff?
- What behavior would replace it well to meet the same need?
- What do you find reinforcing or rewarding that will increase the new behavior?
- What incremental goal can you set that is specific, measurable, achievable, relevant and timely?

SMART
- ✓ Specific (What will I do?)
- ✓ Measurable (How can I consistently measure it?)
- ✓ Achievable (Is it realistic?)

- ✓ Relevant (How does this goal directly relate back to a need?)
- ✓ Time-Bound (When do I want to have this accomplished?)

Start small. When you are successful, you can use your momentum to reset the goal and move forward again.

PULLING IT ALL TOGETHER

I started this book with a story about me. My child was in the ER, I was in a panic, and I didn't know what to do. As I am finishing this story, I would like to tell you that he is on the other side of his illness. But I can't.

My child is still sick. It's two steps forward, one step back. Sometimes it's one step forward and two steps back.

I can't heal his illness. I am his mom. I need to let his doctors treat the disease.

My child is sick, and I can't change that. So, I have changed me. If I am going to be there for him as his mother, I need to be strong. He needs me to be mentally healthy. I can't pour from an empty cup.

I looked at my life with a critical (but kind) eye. I examined what I needed, moment by moment. I realized my purpose: to nurture and encourage him. And to nurture and encourage you.

I stopped telling my story as though I were the victim. I stopped telling his story as though I were the main character.

I changed the words I used in my head. There were a lot of "musts" that kept me clinging to demands that I, that no one, could meet.

I have made some mistakes over the past few years. My chest aches when I think of them. But I am not steeping in regret. I am using my failures to springboard into being a more capable support to him. I can fail, and when I fail, I can learn.

I have asked him repeatedly if it is okay for me to share some of his story, and each time he has responded, "Sure. If you tell my story, others will feel less alone." We can use it for our post-traumatic growth.

Because I had to relearn my role as "mom," I could not be the expert in his illness. I had to ask for help from others.

He currently has five professionals on his mental health team. They collaborate on his treatment. The team provides therapy, holds him accountable for medication compliance, and they provide vocational/educational support. My daughter and I have our own therapists for support, and we have a family therapist (good ole Rog) to work through some hard collective trauma. Social support has also become a lifeline to us.

Finally, I set out a couple goals to help my own mental health. I practice morning devotions, morning pages, meditation, and I have increased my exercise regimen.

I am not perfect, but I am stronger than I was before he got sick.

And I thank you for this. Writing this book for you continues to bring me further in my own journey.

Your Story

You, my beloved friend, are the main character of this final story. As you have read these chapters, you have answered some hard questions.

Remember that perfection has never been the goal here. But I am curious where you can see your improvement over the course of this book.

Have you had an insight? Have you found yourself writing in response to one of the questions? Have you had to put the book down, thinking, "Oof, she just got me there?"

This is what I hope for you. I don't want you conquering all of the facets, answering every question. I want you to see growth in one little area.

Presence:

Are you becoming a little more present? More aware? Have you found ways that you can savor life? Ways you can be grateful?

Purpose:

Are you more aware of what gives your life purpose? Are you prioritizing those motivations? Are you giving yourself time and energy toward the things, activities, or people that bring your life meaning?

Passion:

What do you need? Are you fighting for your survival? Do you need greater safety? Do you need to love yourself? Are you giving in to your passions? If you are doing things that don't align with your deepest needs or your highest aspirations, can you work toward eliminating them?

Plot:
How are you telling your story? Are you chronicling your life with more grace, understanding, kindness? Are you highlighting your strength, your victories?

Perspective:
What are you saying to yourself inside your own head? Are you replacing harsh words with something kinder? Are you speaking to yourself with gentler, more compassionate language?

Perfectionism:
Are you releasing expectations of perfection? Are you allowing yourself to have preferences rather than harsh demands or rigid "musts"? Are you able to say, "I could" rather than "I should"?

Post-Traumatic Growth:
Where have you experienced trauma? And how have you over-come it? What has contributed to your resilience? How have you grown? Have you seen where you are stronger or more powerful because of what you've endured?

Power:
As you move forward, what is the most powerful thing you can do? When you think about how you want your life to be, what strengths can you use to accomplish this? What have you done well in the past that can move you toward that stronger, more intentional future?

People:
Have you found your people, the place where you belong? Do you know who to call upon when you need support, who to call

when you need to celebrate? Who do you trust, and are you that person for others?

Plan:
Finally, can you set forth a plan? What is a small but SMART goal you can use to start?

Each one of these questions holds a nutrient, a nourishment, a supplement to enhance your mental health. Effecting a change in even one of these areas will give you emotional immunity to support your mental functioning.

You are the hero of this story, my dear friend. You have the power to change, to grow, to be your best self. You have control over enhancing your mental health.

Your mental health matters.

ACKNOWLEDGMENTS

A book can only be written with the assistance of many people. My students who have listened attentively, smiled, and nodded as I attempted to teach them these theories. My audiences who have asked questions for which I sought answers. My clients who have put these theories to the test. My friends who distract me with laughter. My family who loves me wholeheartedly. My gratitude goes out to Jackie, my editor, who is a great encourager. Thanks to my publisher, Ann, who has worked tirelessly to get this book out there. Cheers to Abby Anderson, who takes photos that look much better than reality. Thanks to my daughter, who is an enthusiastic cheerleader. I couldn't have done any of this if my sister hadn't insisted I was capable. My spouse deserves credit for graciously enduring my musings, insecurities, and tedious conversations, as well as the many early mornings and late nights that accompanied writing a book like this. Also, thanks for the endless supply of Nerds Clusters.

Finally, I am thankful for the people whose stories I've told here. I am especially grateful to my child who, when asked if I could share our personal story, said, "Yes. We have to talk about it. When it comes to mental health stigma, silence can be deadly."

MENTAL HEALTH RESOURCES

I f you are having a mental health crisis or feel this is an emergency, call 911. If you are having suicidal ideation, call or text 988.

To find a therapist, you can ask for a referral from your physician. You can ask your employer if there is an Employee Assistance Program through your work. You can also look at your insurance provider's website to see who is covered by your plan.

Below are additional resources.

Suicidality:

Are you in crisis? Call or text <u>988</u> or text TALK to <u>741741</u>.

American Foundation for Suicide

Prevention "Whether you have struggled with suicide yourself or have lost a loved one, know you are not alone."
https://afsp.org/

Psychology Today's "Find a Therapist"

This resource provides a search engine to assist you in finding a therapist in your area. You can enter your zip code to start, and then use the drop-down options to narrow your search by issue, insurance, gender, type of therapy, age, price, ethnicity, sexuality, language, and even faith.
https://www.psychologytoday.com/us

Substance Abuse and Mental Health Services Administration (SAMHSA)

"This link is a confidential and anonymous source of information for persons seeking treatment facilities in the United States or U.S. Territories for substance use/addiction and/or mental health problems."

https://www.findtreatment.samhsa.gov/

Black Mental Health Alliance

"The Mission: To develop, promote and sponsor trusted culturally-relevant educational forums, trainings and referral services that support the health and well-being of Black people and their communities." **http://blackmentalhealth.com/**

National Alliance on Mental Illness; Identity and Cultural Dimensions

"Our culture, beliefs, sexual identity, values, race and language all affect how we perceive and experience mental health conditions. In fact, cultural differences can influence what treatments, coping mechanisms and supports work for us. It is therefore *essential* for culture and identity to be a part of the conversation."
https://www.nami.org/Your-Journey/Identity-and-Cultural-Dimensions

National Domestic Violence Hotline

"24 hours a day, seven days a week, 365 days a year, the National Domestic Violence Hotline provides essential tools and support to help survivors of domestic violence so they can live their lives free of abuse."
https://www.thehotline.org/

Rural Mental Health Information

     "While the prevalence of mental illness is similar between rural and urban residents, the services available can be very different. Mental healthcare needs are often not met in many rural communities across the country because adequate services are not present."

https://www.ruralhealthinfo.org/topics/mental-health

REFERENCES

Adler, A. (1929). *The practice and theory of individual psychology*. 2nd edition revised. London/New York, Routledge & K. Paul.

Beck, A. T. (1976). *Cognitive therapy and the emotional disorders*. New York, International Universities Press.

Beck, J. S. (1995). *Cognitive therapy: basics and beyond*. New York, Guilford Press.

Brown, B. (2010). *The gifts of imperfection: let go of who you think you're supposed to be and embrace who you are*. Center City, Minnesota, Hazelden Publishing.

Cameron, J. (2016). *The artist's way: a spiritual path to higher creativity.* 25th anniversary edition. New York, New York, Tarcher Perigee.

De Shazer, Steve. (1985). *Keys to solution in brief therapy* (1st ed.). W.W. Norton.

Ellis, A. (2004). *Rational emotive behavior therapy: It works for me--it can work for you*. Prometheus Books.

Ellis, A., & Joffe-Ellis, D. (2011). *Rational emotive behavior therapy.* First edition. Washington, DC, American Psychological Association.

Elsagher, B. (2003). *If the Battle is Over, Why am I Still in Uniform?* Expert Publishing, Inc.

Ellis, A. (1996;2013;1995;). Better, deeper, and more enduring brief therapy: The rational emotive behavior therapy approach (1st ed.). Brunner/Mazel Publishers.

Fiorini, L. G., Bokanowski, T., Lewkowicz, S., & Person, E. S. (2009). *On Freud's "mourning and melancholia".* London, Karnac.

Frankl, V. E. 1. (2006). *Man's search for meaning.* Boston, Beacon Press.

García, H., Miralles, F., & Cleary, H. (2017*). Ikigai: the Japanese secret to a long and happy life.* New York, Penguin Books.

Garner, J. D., & Enns, C. Z. (2004). *Feminist theories and feminist psychotherapies: origins, themes, and diversity* (2nd ed., pp. vii–vii). Routledge.

Glasser, W. (1998). Choice theory: A new psychology of personal freedom (First ed.). HarperCollinsPublishers.

Heinlein, Robert A. (1973). *Time enough for love, the lives of Lazarus Long; a novel.* New York: Putnam.

Horney, K. (1991). Neurosis and human growth: The struggle toward self-realization. Norton.

Kieth, J. (2022). *Fixing the Funny Bone.* Kindle Direct Publishing.

Klien, A. (1989). *The Healing Power of Humor.* Jeremy Tarcher, Inc.

Lamott, A. (1999). Traveling mercies: some thoughts on faith. 1st edition. New York, Pantheon Books.

Madigan, S. (2011). *Narrative therapy* (1st ed.). American Psychological Association.

Maslow, A. H. (1970). Motivation and personality (Second ed.). Harper & Row.

Meichenbaum, D. (1977). Cognitive-behavior modification: An integrative approach. Plenum Press.

Monk, G. (1997). *Narrative therapy in practice: the archaeology of hope* (1st ed.). Jossey-Bass Publishers.

Mook, D. G. (2004). *Classic experiments in psychology.* Greenwood Press.

Nathan, P. E., Enns, C. Zerbe., & Williams, E. Nutt. (2013). *The Oxford handbook of feminist multicultural counseling psychology.* Oxford University Press.

Nietzsche, F. W., & Large, D. (1998). *Twilight of the idols, or, How to philosophize with a hammer.* Oxford; New York, Oxford University Press.

Perls, F. S., & Perls, F. S. (1973). *The gestalt approach & Eyewitness to therapy.* [Ben Lomond, California], Science & Behavior Books.

Skinner, B. F. 1. (1953). *Science and human behavior.* New York, Macmillan.

Tarvin, A. (2019). *Humor That Works: The missing skill for success and happiness at work.* Kindle Direct Publishing.

Tronick, E. Z., Als, H., Adamson, L., Wise, S., & Brazelton, T. B. (1978). The infant's response to entrapment between contradictory messages in face-to-face interaction. Journal of the American Academy of Child Psychiatry, 17, 1-13.

Tronick, E. Z., Als, H., & Brazelton, T. B. (1980). Monadic phases: A structural descriptive analysis of infant-mother face-to-face interaction. Merrill-Palmer Quarterly of Behavior and Development, 26, 1-24.